Pondering
the Parables

What in the World was Jesus Thinking?

RAY SANDERS

LUCIDBOOKS

Pondering the Parables
What in the World was Jesus Thinking?
Copyright © 2025 by Ray Sanders

Published by Lucid Books in Houston, TX
www.LucidBooks.com

ISBN: 978-1-63296-816-6
eISBN: 978-1-63296-817-3

Special Sales: Most Lucid Books titles are available in special quantity discounts. Custom imprinting or excerpting can also be done to fit special needs. Contact Lucid Books at Info@LucidBooks.com

To Stephanie.

You are my biggest fan, cheerleader, and confidant. You are my best friend, the love of my life, and the one I am privileged to call my wife. Without your encouragement and support, this book would have remained a good intention. Because of you, I have stepped out, bared my soul, and opened my heart to all who care to read this little bundle of words.

Thank you, Stephanie. You are my everything. You share in this labor of love. It is dedicated to you and the Lord we love.

Jesus always used stories and illustrations like these when speaking to the crowds. In fact, He never spoke to them without using such parables. This fulfilled what God had spoken through the prophet:

> *"I will speak to you in parables.*
> *I will explain things hidden since the creation of the world."*
>
> —Matthew 13:34–35

Table of Contents

Introduction: What in the World was Jesus Thinking? 1

Day 1: From the Inside Out 3

Day 2: Illumination 6

Day 3: The Rock 9

Day 4: The Magnitude of Such Love! 13

Day 5: While the Getting Is Good 16

Day 6: Ready? 20

Day 7: The Gift of Leadership 24

Day 8: When "Ughs" Come 28

Day 9: 100x 32

Day 10: Weeds and Seeds 36

Day 11: A Mysterious Journey 40

Day 12: Together on Purpose 43

Day 13: The Proof is in the Making 46

Day 14: The Great Discovery 49

Day 15: Behold the Beloved 52

Day 16: The Keepers 55

Day 17: Nailed It 59

Day 18: Sheep, a Shepherd, and a Thief 62

Day 19: Come Home 67

Day 20: When Duty Calls   70

Day 21: Believing in You   73

Day 22: Ours to Render   77

Day 23: A Tale of Three Friends   81

Day 24: Party Hardy   85

Day 25: Excuse Me   89

Day 26: Count the Cost   93

Day 27: Regain and Retain   96

Day 28: Time to Party   99

Day 29: Loosen Your Grip   104

Day 30: Carried or Buried?   109

Day 31: The Time is Now   113

Day 32: Two Ears and One Mouth   118

Day 33: Embrace Humility   122

Day 34: Listen Up   125

Day 35: Walk the Talk   130

Day 36: Taking Advantage?   134

Day 37: Hard-Hearted, Half-Hearted, or Wholehearted?   139

Day 38: Fig-ure It Out!   143

Day 39: Aware and Prepared   146

Day 40: When Did We?   150

Acknowledgments   155

About the Author   157

What in the World was Jesus Thinking?

This little book originated when a few friends encouraged me to spend some time focusing on the parables of Jesus. The idea was to approach the parables as if I were there listening to Jesus share them for the very first time. As I did this, I often found myself asking, *What in the world was Jesus thinking?* His parables were simple, yet complex; short, yet powerful. I discovered Jesus was a master storyteller, and the stories He told made me think and had a lasting impact on my life.

I make no theological claim regarding my ponderings on Jesus's parables. What I share with you in the pages that follow are simply my personal thoughts based on the lessons I learned sitting at the feet of Jesus for forty days through the Scriptures. I have found Jesus's approach fascinating and effective. For me, His principles reach across time and remain as relevant today as the day they were first spoken.

As you embark on this adventure of sitting at the feet of Jesus, why not consider asking some friends to join you? As you ponder the words of Jesus and their impact on your life, jot down your takeaways and discuss your thoughts (and mine) with friends in a small group, over a cup of coffee, on a regular conference call, or even in a group text message. These words are alive! Don't be surprised to hear a variety of perspectives—the Scriptures speak to everyone in a very personal way.

Jesus's parables have given me reason for pause. Your experience will likely be different from your friends' experiences and mine. Therein lies the beauty and the mystery of Jesus and his parables.

I have done my best to present the readings in chronological order as Jesus may have shared them. While His parables are easily crossed-referenced, I have chosen to take a single passage approach. I have found reading one parable a day to be inspirational and life-changing.

I am certain you will enjoy the journey as you, too, sit at the feet of the master storyteller and ponder, *What in the world was Jesus thinking?*

PS: I would love to hear what you discover as you spend time pondering the parables of Jesus. Please send your thoughts to me at ray@raysanders.com.

From the Inside Out

When I was a little boy, I had a favorite western shirt. People must have thought my family was dirt-poor because I wore it everywhere and nearly every day.

But then the unthinkable started happening: The fabric began to loosen, and the threads began to fray! How could this be? A tiny tear appeared and, before too long, my comfy little shirt (with the coolest pearl buttons) was beyond repair. The pain was real!

Who hasn't owned a favorite shirt or a perfect-fitting pair of jeans they hoped would last forever? We can try to patch up the holes to make it last a little longer, but we know the clothing will never be the same. It's inevitable that it's time for something new.

Jesus says that no one patches old clothes with new cloth because it only leads to bigger tears when the new cloth shrinks and pulls away. In the same way, He says that *"no one puts new wine in old wineskins.*" Why not? Because the risk of the old wineskins bursting and wasting the new wine is simply too high. The old wineskins have fulfilled their role. If new wine is to ever reach its full potential, new wineskins will be required.

In a similar way, when we're bursting with new ideas or innovations, sometimes we need new environments too. If you force something new into an old system, things could fall apart. If you stay too long, the dream could die. You might have to make a change in order to reach your full potential.

Old ways have a way of hanging on by a thread, but Jesus proposes an option better than anything we have ever experienced. Rather than hanging on too long or trying to force something new into something old, Jesus knows we need a new beginning.

Jesus isn't a fan of patches—He wants to clothe us with a permanent solution. If we are willing, He'll change us from the inside out.

> *"Besides, who would patch old clothing with new cloth? For the new patch would shrink and rip away from the old cloth, leaving an even bigger tear than before.*
>
> *"And no one puts new wine into old wineskins. For the old skins would burst from the pressure, spilling the wine and ruining the skins. New wine is stored in new wineskins so that both are preserved."*
>
> —Matthew 9:16–17

PAUSE & PONDER:
RECORD YOUR REFLECTIONS AND PERSONAL INSIGHTS

Is there an area of your life where you're hanging on too long? What would it look like to let go and ask Jesus to change you from the inside out?

DAY 2:

Illumination

One of the wonderful things about sleeping outside is the discovery of God's magnificent display of stars. These glistening celestial jewels of the great unknown are often overlooked by inhabitants of the concrete jungle.

I'll always remember a drive I took with my eldest son to the far northwest corner of Oklahoma. It was not just flat, it was *really* flat! Like the Sackett brothers from Louis L'Amour's western novels, we discovered amazing sunsets and the beauty of the galaxy as we rested on the hood of my car in the middle of the prairie. With crickets chirping in the background, we felt a slight southern breeze as we lay in wonder of it all.

We sometimes forget that Jesus lived on the road and slept in tents or outside by the light of the moon. I wonder if He couldn't imagine falling asleep staring at a ceiling when God's creation provided an ever-changing kaleidoscope just after sundown.

Jesus tells His followers they are the light of the world. They are like the stars— twinkling little lights contributing to the ambience of a divine experience. Could there be a more beautiful compliment?

Jesus goes on to say that His disciples are *"like a city on a hilltop that cannot be hidden."* He had no doubt slept on the outskirts of many towns and observed the flickering lights of candles in the homes of people He so desperately loved. I like to imagine the anticipation of visiting them filled His heart as He gently fell asleep under the blanket of God's heavenly masterpiece.

It's a beautiful picture, no doubt. But the world remains a predominantly dark place, and not just when the sun slides below the horizon or on a moonless night. No, the world can be dark and gloomy at any time of day or night. Evil lurks among us bringing sadness, hurt, and fear.

People are in need of hope. For many, life is a dark dungeon of despair. Troubles, worries, setbacks, sickness, and pain are constant reminders that something is terribly wrong. This is not life as it was meant to be.

Jesus is the light that shines within every believer to bring hope to the world. He encourages His followers to let their light shine. Don't hide it! Let your light sparkle! Bring Jesus to the world to illuminate the darkness.

God is love. Love is the fuel, the power, and the energy that illuminates us. Spread the love. Push back the darkness. Shine the light.

> *"You are the light of the world—like a city on a hilltop that cannot be hidden. No one lights a lamp and then puts it under a basket. Instead, a lamp is placed on a stand, where it gives light to everyone in the house."*
> —Matthew 5:14–15

PAUSE & PONDER:
RECORD YOUR REFLECTIONS AND PERSONAL INSIGHTS

Who in your life is experiencing darkness? What's one way you could be a light to that person?

DAY 3:

The Rock

When I was in high school, I took a job as a carpenter's assistant. The first day on the job the foreman sent me looking for a "sky hook." Not wanting to be embarrassed, I climbed down from the rafters and made my way to the toolbox. After taking out nearly every tool in search of something that might resemble a "sky hook," I realized I had been duped! Rookie mistake. I had been officially initiated, and I learned my lesson: If you don't know, ask!

Jesus says, *"Anyone who listens to my teaching and follows it is wise, like a person who builds a house on solid rock"* (Matt. 7:24).

It should not surprise us that Jesus has an excellent perspective on building better lives. Jesus grew up as a carpenter who fabricated foundations for houses by shaping beams from raw timber and moving heavy boulders by hand. He was well-acquainted with the skills and materials needed to build a strong foundation. For those who listen to and obey His message, Jesus becomes the bedrock, the foundation, for wise and abundant living!

However, Jesus also says, *"But anyone who hears my teaching and doesn't obey it is foolish, like a person who builds a house on sand"* (Matt. 7:26).

"In one ear and out the other" describes people who attend a conference, lecture, or religious service only to occupy a seat. The same could be said of those who read books, listen to podcasts, and watch videos but never act on the insights revealed. They are hearing but not listening. They are not taking what they've heard to heart.

For those who aren't listening and those who are too proud to accept His teachings, Jesus proves to be a stumbling block. When our lives are built on self-help principles, positive thinking, or mystical notions, Jesus warns that we stand on sinking sand. He says, *"When the rains and floods come and the winds beat against that house, it will collapse with a mighty crash"* (Matt. 7:27).

But if we build our lives on Jesus's teachings, we'll be able to get through the torrential rains, gusty winds, and painful trials of our lives. We can endure any storm with confidence, knowing our lives are built on solid ground.

Sweet Jesus, the strong and competent carpenter. Joseph's boy from the little town of Bethlehem. Mary's precious child. Our Lord. Our Savior. God's Son. Jesus is the cornerstone that holds everything in life together. He is the rock of our salvation, the foundation on which we stand.

"Anyone who listens to my teaching and follows it is wise, like a person who builds a house on solid rock. Though the rain comes in torrents and the floodwaters rise and the winds beat against that house, it won't collapse because it is built on bedrock. But anyone who hears my teaching and doesn't obey it is foolish, like a person who builds a house on sand. When the rains and floods come and the winds beat against that house, it will collapse with a mighty crash."

—Matthew 7:24–27

PAUSE & PONDER:
RECORD YOUR REFLECTIONS AND PERSONAL INSIGHTS

What in the world was Jesus thinking when He told this parable? Where is God inviting you to listen to Him?

The Magnitude of Such Love!

There is an old saying in the southern part of the United States that goes something like this: "If you ever come upon a turtle on a post, you know he didn't get there alone."

When you think about it, we are all turtles on posts. No one gets to where they are on their own. None of us are really self-made. If nothing else, we owe a debt of gratitude to those who have helped us along the way. The power of influence often comes from a teacher, coach, friend, coworker, mentor, sibling, minister, parent, or perhaps even a complete stranger. We all have ordinary angels who have helped make us who we are today.

Jesus tells a story of a lender who extends loans to two different men. As good as their intentions may have been to repay their debts, they fail. Both men come up short—they miss the mark and default on their loans.

Amazingly, the lender has mercy and cancels their debts entirely. Not one penny owed! He forgives them and ultimately pays the price for their shortfalls.

We find ourselves in a similar predicament. We can have the best of intentions and give it our all, but in the end, our sincere efforts fall short. On our own, we will never meet the requirements for heaven's reward.

But the good news is truly good news. Jesus stepped in when we were out of options. He paid the price for our failures. We came up short, but when we accept His mercy, our debt is paid in full. We are set free.

However, freedom is not free. Whether it's a lender who covers a borrower's debt or the Savior who covers our sins, there is a price for freedom. Debts still have to be paid. Those who have had their debts paid overflow with love and gratitude for the one who lightened their load. Oh, the magnitude of such love!

> *Then Jesus told him this story: "A man loaned money to two people—500 pieces of silver to one and 50 pieces to the other. But neither of them could repay him, so he kindly forgave them both, canceling their debts. Who do you suppose loved him more after that?"*
> —Luke 7:41–42

PAUSE & PONDER:
RECORD YOUR REFLECTIONS AND PERSONAL INSIGHTS

Think about someone to whom you owe a debt of gratitude. What did it cost that person to serve you? How can you extend that kind of love to someone else?

DAY 5:

While the Getting Is Good

I have a confession to make. There was a time in my life when I was fairly concerned with the type of vehicle I drove. It wasn't a matter of function; it was purely a matter of fashion. I believed the car I drove was important to the image I wanted to maintain.

Eventually, I realized my need for a great-looking set of wheels was really an indication I was suffering from a poor self-image. I decided to drive my old truck—hail damage and all—until I no longer cared about what other people thought about my mode of transportation. It took longer than you might think. But as the odometer on my old wagon rolled past zero (a few times), I decided to graduate to a new car, free of zip ties, baling wire, and duct tape!

How is life measured? When our story ends, how will we know if we got the most out of life? As humans, we have a desire to acquire. To get it while the getting is good. But what are we out to get? For some it is an education, a spouse, a good job, more stuff, and more money. Yeah, money! As they say, "There aren't too many problems that money won't fix." Well, not so fast. This is where we start getting into trouble.

Jesus challenges our way of thinking. He's not against money. Even Jesus had a treasurer. Clearly money is an important part of life and ministry. But a closer look reveals Jesus wasn't worried about whether He rode a late model mule, lived in a large hut, or wore the latest threads from Jerusalem's high-fashion district.

For Jesus, life is measured by relationships, not possessions. He believes a quality relationship with God leads to great relationships with others. He sums up all of Scripture with the command to love God and others as we love ourselves. There is no mention of loving money or belongings.

Jesus challenges us to fill up storehouses in heaven. Relationships are the only currency that will transfer to eternity. No wonder He says, *"A person is a fool to store up earthly wealth but not have a rich relationship with God"* (Luke 12:21). Jesus has a heart for people. For Him, life is measured by rich relationships not earthly wealth. Let's get those while the getting is good!

> *Then he said, "Beware! Guard against every kind of greed. Life is not measured by how much you own."*
>
> *Then he told them a story: "A rich man had a fertile farm that produced fine crops. He said to himself, 'What should I do? I don't have room for all my crops.' Then he said, 'I know! I'll tear down my barns*

and build bigger ones. Then I'll have room enough to store all my wheat and other goods. And I'll sit back and say to myself, "My friend, you have enough stored away for years to come. Now take it easy! Eat, drink, and be merry!"'

"But God said to him, 'You fool! You will die this very night. Then who will get everything you worked for?'

"Yes, a person is a fool to store up earthly wealth but not have a rich relationship with God."

—Luke 12:15–21

PAUSE & PONDER:
RECORD YOUR REFLECTIONS AND PERSONAL INSIGHTS

What are you valuing most right now? What would it look like to release that thing and prioritize rich relationships instead?

DAY 6:

Ready?

On your mark, get set, go! Who doesn't recall the anticipation of hearing these words before a good footrace as a kid? Surprisingly, these simple little words also serve as a big reminder as we run the race of life today.

Finding the mark is challenging. Getting set rattles our nerves. But one thing we can count on is this: Unless we are ready, we won't be prepared when it's time to go.

On a recent trip to Africa, a friend of mine, who was the president of a university, lost his luggage in transit. We left the airport empty-handed, doubting we would ever see his suitcase again. Yet early in the morning, a pair of young men knocked on his door with his luggage in tow. As an expression of his gratitude, my friend offered the couriers a handsome tip. Much to his surprise, they declined. He then offered them a full scholarship to his university. Yet again, they declined. After learning they already had undergraduate degrees, my friend offered them graduate degrees instead. Now that was an offer they couldn't resist!

Because those two men were prepared, they were in the perfect position to take advantage of an incredible, life-changing opportunity. Their commitment to getting an education and their servant hearts paid rich returns. When the time came, they were ready to go.

Jesus encourages us to be ready. He wants us to be fit to serve in the same way that an athlete has conditioned his body and mind to run a race. He wants us to be prepared to pour our lives into others.

We are called to be servants. We aren't called to be sluggards. We are called to put on an apron, roll up our sleeves, and serve. Being ready means doing our homework, thinking ahead, taking initiative, being intentional, having a servant attitude, and looking for opportunities to be the hands and feet of Jesus.

Winning the race is in the preparation. Success is in the details. Failing to plan is planning to fail. Being ready helps us reach our full potential.

When we are ready as Jesus challenges us to be, we will be found serving and looking. Jesus will no doubt return riding on the clouds someday, but He also shows up daily when we least expect it in the eyes of a child, in the request of a friend, and in the needs of a total stranger (Matt. 25:36–40).

Are you ready to be of service? On your mark. Get set. Go!

"Be dressed for service and keep your lamps burning, as though you were waiting for your master to return from the wedding feast. Then you will be ready to open the door and let him in the moment he arrives and knocks. The servants who are ready and waiting

for his return will be rewarded. I tell you the truth, he himself will seat them, put on an apron, and serve them as they sit and eat! He may come in the middle of the night or just before dawn. But whenever he comes, he will reward the servants who are ready.

"Understand this: If a homeowner knew exactly when a burglar was coming, he would not permit his house to be broken into. You also must be ready all the time, for the Son of Man will come when least expected."

—Luke 12:35–40

PAUSE & PONDER:
RECORD YOUR REFLECTIONS AND PERSONAL INSIGHTS

Are you actively looking and preparing for opportunities to serve other people? If so, how? If not, why not?

The Gift of Leadership

Being a leader is not a given. True leadership is not based on position or pedigree—it's based on influence. Leadership is a gift that requires the leader to be responsible and encouraging to others. A true leader is someone people willingly follow. A leader with no followers is just on a good walk.

Have you ever known a leader who wasn't fit to lead? Jesus indicates that a faithful and sensible servant is given leadership roles. These criteria are indicators that the leader has influence. Failing to be a faithful and sensible servant has disqualified many in the position of leadership from being among the best.

To be faithful is to be predictable in a good way. Good leaders can be counted on. They do what they say. They come through on their promises. They are people of their word. They are faithful.

Great leaders are also sensible servants. They know when the team needs support, and they know when to bring a healthy dose of challenge. The best leaders lead with love. When they do, mercy and grace follow. They aren't pushovers—they are firm but reasonable.

To whom much has been given, much is required. It has been said that the reward for good work is more work! Such is the case for the servant leader. Any seasoned leader knows that being the leader can be lonely. The headlines are not always favorable, and you are not always everyone's best friend. Nonetheless, leaders can expect a reward for their good work. The satisfaction of a job well done has carried many leaders to the next level of service.

The key to effective leadership is to lead with love as a faithful and sensible servant. Leadership is a gift, a responsibility, and an opportunity to serve. Are you a leader worth following?

> *And the Lord replied, "A faithful, sensible servant is one to whom the master can give the responsibility of managing his other household servants and feeding them. If the master returns and finds that the servant has done a good job, there will be a reward. I tell you the truth, the master will put that servant in charge of all he owns. But what if the servant thinks, 'My master won't be back for a while,' and he begins beating the other servants, partying, and getting drunk? The master will return unannounced and unexpected, and he will cut the servant in pieces and banish him with the unfaithful.*

"And a servant who knows what the master wants, but isn't prepared and doesn't carry out those instructions, will be severely punished. But someone who does not know, and then does something wrong, will be punished only lightly. When someone has been given much, much will be required in return; and when someone has been entrusted with much, even more will be required."

—Luke 12:42–48

PAUSE & PONDER:
RECORD YOUR REFLECTIONS AND PERSONAL INSIGHTS

Think about the best leaders you've known. What qualities made them worth following? How can you incorporate those qualities in your own leadership opportunities?

DAY 8:

When "Ughs" Come

There is a popular clothing line that sports the phrase, "Life is good." This optimistic little saying serves as a great reminder when things are going our way in life. Encouraging attitudes pop up in other phrases as well. "Be positive." "Chin up." "Attitude is everything." "Smile!" These little reminders can make a big difference in the way we see and walk through life.

There are times when we feel as if everything is going our way. Life isn't just good; it's great. Spirits are running high. Nothing could be better. The bank account is full, and wherever we go, we feel the love! When that's true of your life, let the good times roll! Keep them coming for as long as you can because one thing is certain: While things are good, life's "ughs" are coming.

Jesus tells a story about a man who plants a fig tree in his garden. While there is much we can learn from this parable, what stands out to me is the idea of *disappointment*. When the man in the story goes to check on the fig tree, Jesus says he is *"always disappointed."* Ugh. I can relate to that feeling, can't you? Oh, the weight of it all. Those ugly realities—big and small—reminding us that not everything goes our way. Things we hoped for and worked for vanish before our very eyes. Teams disappoint, jobs disappoint, and relationships disappoint. We even disappoint ourselves. There is no shortage of setbacks in life.

When life disappoints us, what should we do? Should we try harder? Give it a second chance? Suffer through it? Hang on? Or let go? The answer is: It depends.

There are no easy answers for when life lets us down. But when it does, we do well to remind ourselves that despite life's disappointments, there is Someone who never disappoints. He loves us through it all. He has been there Himself, and while He may or may not take away the pain, He will be with us—comforting us and caring about the hurts, let downs, and regrets.

When life disappoints us, it helps to know that the Lord understands. He is with us through it all. Life isn't always good, but God is.

> *Then Jesus told this story: "A man planted a fig tree in his garden and came again and again to see if there was any fruit on it, but he was always disappointed. Finally, he said to his gardener, 'I've waited three years, and there hasn't been a single fig! Cut it down. It's just taking up space in the garden.'*

"The gardener answered, 'Sir, give it one more chance. Leave it another year, and I'll give it special attention and plenty of fertilizer. If we get figs next year, fine. If not, then you can cut it down.'"

—Luke 13:6–9

PAUSE & PONDER:
RECORD YOUR REFLECTIONS AND PERSONAL INSIGHTS

What disappointments—"ughs"—are you facing in life right now? How does believing God is with you impact your perspective?

100x

I had a young friend who moved from a developing nation to study in the US. One day as we were filling my car with gas, I asked him to use a squeegee to clean my windshield. It quickly became obvious that he had never done this before, and the more he cleaned, the worse things got. I was willing to help, but he never looked up, so I watched and waited as he continued to work.

A line grew behind us, and impatient customers started honking. Finally, he looked at me in desperation. He was ready to accept help. With a few simple adjustments to his technique, the windshield was clean, and we were on our way.

You've likely heard these sayings: "That dog won't hunt!" "You can lead a horse to water, but you can't make him drink." "When the student is ready, the teacher will appear." What are they all getting at? In essence, sometimes trying to teach someone is a waste of time. It's not that the instructor isn't present, willing, and able to teach. No, it's that the student is unwilling to listen and learn. Everyone makes mistakes, but to intentionally refuse instruction and guidance is a choice. And choices have consequences.

Being a teachable student who is attentive and willing to listen results in growth and greater satisfaction in life. Jesus wants us to consider the return on our investment. He says it this way, *"Still other seeds fell on fertile soil, and they sprouted, grew, and produced a crop that was thirty, sixty, and even a hundred times as much as had been planted!"* (Mark 4: 8). There is an obvious reward for being fertile soil—for being eager to listen and learn.

To someone who is unwilling to listen, wisdom sounds like noise. Words of wisdom only have meaning when we listen to understand. We would do well to recognize how pride, the cares of this world, the lure of wealth, and the desire for nicer things often distract us from the life-changing message of Jesus. We may hear what the Lord is saying, but we will not understand the depth of what He is teaching until we are willing to truly listen. When we do, we will reap the benefits of such insight one hundredfold!

> *Listen! A farmer went out to plant some seed. As he scattered it across his field, some of the seed fell on a footpath, and the birds came and ate it. Other seed fell on shallow soil with underlying rock. The seed sprouted quickly because the soil was shallow. But the plant soon wilted under the hot sun, and since it didn't have deep roots, it died. Other seed fell among thorns that grew up and choked out the tender plants*

so they produced no grain. Still other seeds fell on fertile soil, and they sprouted, grew, and produced a crop that was thirty, sixty, and even a hundred times as much as had been planted! . . .

The farmer plants seed by taking God's word to others. The seed that fell on the footpath represents those who hear the message, only to have Satan come at once and take it away. The seed on the rocky soil represents those who hear the message and immediately receive it with joy. But since they don't have deep roots, they don't last long. They fall away as soon as they have problems or are persecuted for believing God's word. The seed that fell among the thorns represents others who hear God's word, but all too quickly the message is crowded out by the worries of this life, the lure of wealth, and the desire for other things, so no fruit is produced. And the seed that fell on good soil represents those who hear and accept God's word and produce a harvest of thirty, sixty, or even a hundred times as much as had been planted!

—Mark 4:3–8, 14–20

PAUSE & PONDER:
RECORD YOUR REFLECTIONS AND PERSONAL INSIGHTS

Think of a time when someone shared wisdom with you, but you chose not to listen. What was the result? How is Jesus speaking to you today?

Weeds and Seeds

We live in a world of polar opposites. Like oil and water, good and evil simply don't mix. When it comes to deciding whether we're going to follow God or the world around us, the stakes are high. We aren't tossing a salad. We are in a battle for our lives. The choices we make in this life have eternal ramifications.

Let's be clear and of sober minds: Good and evil are competing for the fertile soil of our hearts. Healthy plants and invasive weeds sprout from the same field. All of us, God's people as well as those who are far from him, share common space on this spinning blue ball floating among the stars. Like it or not, we are in this together.

You may be asking, "Can't we all just get along? What about live and let live?" That sounds nice in theory, but it's not reality. The farmer can't just pretend that he'll sell the weeds alongside the wheat. When it's time for the harvest, the crops will be gathered, and the weeds will be destroyed. There is no middle ground—we have to choose between God's truth and the way of the world.

So what are we supposed to do if we find weeds among the seeds? Burn the field? No! Hate is not an option. Our role is not to plow down people who fail to recognize God's love. We must stand our ground and be deeply rooted in the truth, but we must also overflow with love for other people.

We need to remember we are the seeds. We're not the farmer. For the farmer, timing is everything. It is not a matter of *if* but *when*. Evil may have its day in the sun, but the farmer knows the harvest is coming. He will reap good from what he has sown. The evil that tries to rob him will ultimately be plucked from his presence and consumed by the fire of justice. In the meantime, we wait, and we love the *hell* out of our enemies.

When the weeds of evil appear to have taken over, we must stand strong. We can choose to focus our efforts on growing in the warmth of the Son, nurturing the good that is within us, and loving everyone who surrounds us, knowing that all the while harvesttime is coming.

> *Here is another story Jesus told: "The Kingdom of Heaven is like a farmer who planted good seed in his field. But that night as the workers slept, his enemy came and planted weeds among the wheat, then slipped away. When the crop began to grow and produce grain, the weeds also grew.*
>
> *"The farmer's workers went to him and said, 'Sir, the field where you planted that good seed is full of weeds! Where did they come from?'*

*"'An enemy has done this!' the farmer exclaimed.
"'Should we pull out the weeds?' they asked.*

*"'No,' he replied, 'you'll uproot the wheat if you do. Let
both grow together until the harvest. Then I will tell the
harvesters to sort out the weeds, tie them into bundles,
and burn them, and to put the wheat in the barn. . . .'"*

*Then, leaving the crowds outside, Jesus went into the
house. His disciples said, "Please explain to us the story
of the weeds in the field."*

*Jesus replied, "The Son of Man is the farmer who
plants the good seed. The field is the world, and the good
seed represents the people of the Kingdom. The weeds
are the people who belong to the evil one. The enemy
who planted the weeds among the wheat is the devil.
The harvest is the end of the world, and the harvesters
are the angels.*

*"Just as the weeds are sorted out and burned in the
fire, so it will be at the end of the world. The Son of
Man will send his angels, and they will remove from
his Kingdom everything that causes sin and all who
do evil. And the angels will throw them into the fiery
furnace, where there will be weeping and gnashing
of teeth. Then the righteous will shine like the sun in
their Father's Kingdom. Anyone with ears to hear
should listen and understand!"*

—Matthew 13:24–30, 36–43

PAUSE & PONDER:
RECORD YOUR REFLECTIONS AND PERSONAL INSIGHTS

Where is God calling you to stand firm in His truth? How is He asking you to love people who fail to recognize His love?

A Mysterious Journey

Any child who has ever planted a lone bean in a cup of fertile soil can attest to the thrill the experience can bring. The process captivates little minds: "Will today be the day? Will the soil finally crack and reveal what has been developing beneath the surface?" Amazingly, a little water, sunlight, and patience produces incredible results. What was is no longer, as something altogether new and fascinating emerges from the dirt.

There is a certain mystery to the journey a seed takes from the time it is buried beneath the dirt until it grows into a viable plant. The transformation is amazing, and yet it appears nearly automatic.

There is a similar beautiful mystery to the gospel. Once the gospel has been planted in our hearts, it begins to transform who we were into something new and more magnificent.

The Bible tells us that God's Word does not return void (Isa. 55:11). Jesus has a way of taking who we are and turning us into something wonderful. Just as the seed will never be the same once the plant begins to grow, when we embrace the gospel and die to ourselves, the result is a new beginning, a new creation, and a new life all together in Him!

Ah, the mystery of the seed. The mystery of the gospel, indeed!

> *Jesus also said, "The Kingdom of God is like a farmer who scatters seed on the ground. Night and day, while he's asleep or awake, the seed sprouts and grows, but he does not understand how it happens. The earth produces the crops on its own. First a leaf blade pushes through, then the heads of wheat are formed, and finally the grain ripens. And as soon as the grain is ready, the farmer comes and harvests it with a sickle, for the harvest time has come."*
>
> — Mark 4:26–29

PAUSE & PONDER:
RECORD YOUR REFLECTIONS AND PERSONAL INSIGHTS

How have you seen God transform people, including yourself, into something completely new? How is He continuing to change you today?

Together on Purpose

B ig things can come from small beginnings, especially when we work together on purpose with the Lord's blessing. Not everything meets its full potential, but when we have a clear understanding of who we were created to be in cooperation with God and others, we can achieve far more than we imagine. With God at our side, even the most improbable things are possible.

Upon reading the parable of the mustard seed in Luke 13, Apostle Paul's words in 1 Corinthians 3:6–8 take on an even deeper meaning:

> *I planted the seed in your hearts, and Apollos watered it, but it was God who made it grow. It's not important who does the planting, or who does the watering. What's important is that God makes the seed grow. The one who plants and the one who waters work together with the same purpose. And both will be rewarded for their own hard work.*

No one can do everything, but everyone can do something. We can do more together than we ever could alone, especially when we have little concern about who gets the credit.

Each of us has a unique role to play in God's story. We were designed for a specific purpose and calling. When we try to be something we are not, we accomplish less than our best. If we aren't us, who will be? We each have gifts, talents, and abilities that might seem small at times, but when aptly applied, they can yield incredible results.

May we be found doing the work assigned to us, based on our unique abilities, working together according to his purpose, and trusting God to bring forth the produce!

> *Then Jesus said, "What is the Kingdom of God like? How can I illustrate it? It is like a tiny mustard seed that a man planted in a garden; it grows and becomes a tree, and the birds make nests in its branches."*
> —Luke 13:18–19

PAUSE & PONDER:
RECORD YOUR REFLECTIONS AND PERSONAL INSIGHTS

What are some of your unique gifts, talents, and abilities? How might God be asking you to use those for Him?

The Proof is in the Making

Every baker knows that too much or too little of any one ingredient can ruin an otherwise delightful batch of bread. Too little yeast and the bread won't rise. Too much salt and it will be inedible. Adding ingredients in the right proportions and at the appropriate times is the key to a masterful culinary work of art.

When making bread, we mix yeast with flour, salt, and warm water or milk. Then the dough is kneaded and left to rise. Finally, the dough is shaped into loaves and baked at just the right temperature and duration.

Some bread doughs should be knocked back after they rise and then left to rise again. This process is called *proofing*, and longer proof times tend to improve the bread's flavor. However, the yeast can fail to raise the bread in the final stage, which could result in disaster, further illustrating the importance of the baker's knowledge and skill when it comes to the art of bread making.

Sometimes, we might feel the heat of the kitchen or experience being "knocked back" like a ball of dough. Other times, we fail to see the difference little things can make in our lives, and we neglect key ingredients such as prayer and time alone with God.

But God is the master baker. He is using things—big and small—to make us into the works of art we were meant to be. When we learn to rest in God's hands, He keenly shapes the dough of our lives into perfection, yielding a beautiful "loaf" every time. The proof is in the making!

> *Jesus also used this illustration: "The Kingdom of Heaven is like the yeast a woman used in making bread. Even though she put only a little yeast in three measures of flour, it permeated every part of the dough."*
>
> —Matthew 13:33

PAUSE & PONDER:
RECORD YOUR REFLECTIONS AND PERSONAL INSIGHTS

Where have you felt "knocked back" in your life? Even in those hard things, do you see ways God is shaping you?

The Great Discovery

Sometimes, we overlook the fact that the best things in life are often right beneath our feet. They have been there all along but somehow, we missed them. Living in the here and now is frequently overlooked because we set our eyes too far down the road. In our pursuit of the final destination, we fail to experience the joy of the ride today. We are victims of FOMO—fear of missing out. We miss what is for the idea of what might be.

Life becomes a blur as we scurry and hurry from one activity to the next. We choke down fast food and gulp hot coffee, using our knees to steer on life's superhighway. With a wink and a nod to those we love, we collapse into bed at the end of the day trying to make sense of it all, wondering why we do what we do, day in and day out. Anxiety lingers, and thoughts cycle until we are overcome by exhaustion. This is the life! Or is it?

All too often what we desire most is well within our reach, waiting to be discovered. But somehow the life we always wanted gets so crowded out by the doing that we forget about being. In our hunt for treasure, we lose sight of what we are looking for. In our rush, we forget to pause—to linger and breathe in the pleasant aroma of the present. What blessings could be ours for the taking if only we were more aware?

If we are not careful, we will overlook the obvious in our pursuit of all life has to offer. The fullness of a life that was meant to be may soon be crowded out by massive emptiness.

Fortunately, all is not lost. There is One who offers life to the fullest, a life with meaning and purpose. He is the life-giver. The life He gives is well within our reach. It is a gift. It is a treasure waiting to be discovered.

Many weary sojourners have come to discover that life in Jesus is the very thing they seek. Amazingly, the treasure they had hoped for is theirs for the taking. He is the great discovery.

> *"The Kingdom of Heaven is like a treasure that a man discovered hidden in a field. In his excitement, he hid it again and sold everything he owned to get enough money to buy the field."*
>
> —Matthew 13:44

PAUSE & PONDER:
RECORD YOUR REFLECTIONS AND PERSONAL INSIGHTS

What is it that you desire right now? What are some practical ways you can slow down and be more present in your daily life?

Behold the Beloved

Rare and elegant and beautiful, pearls are among some of the most sought-after gemstones in the world. They are both classic and contemporary as a symbol of beauty and purity. Amazingly, natural pearls are the only jewel created by a living animal, and they are found in about one in every ten thousand wild oysters!

While pearls are hard to find, it would be even harder to find a woman anywhere in the world who would not enjoy wearing a strand of gem-quality pearls. Fine jewelers recognize the value we place on pearls, and they are forever on the lookout, searching to bring premium pearls to market from around the world.

As magnificent as pearls may be, we would do well to remember that God is the ultimate jeweler. While we appreciate the beauty of His creation, there is nothing He loves, cherishes, and adores more than us.

Like a diver in search of a rare pearl, Jesus went to great lengths to rescue us from the depths. Incredibly, He paid the price, and we reaped the benefits. He exchanged everything for us when we had nothing to offer in return.

While others may overlook our value, God sees our true worth. We are rare, precious, and beautiful in His sight. We are the jewels in His crown. Behold the beloved, His beautiful strand of pearls.

> *"Again, the Kingdom of Heaven is like a merchant on the lookout for choice pearls. When he discovered a pearl of great value, he sold everything he owned and bought it!"*
>
> —Matthew 13:45–46

PAUSE & PONDER:
RECORD YOUR REFLECTIONS AND PERSONAL INSIGHTS

Do you believe God sees you and values you like a rare jewel?
How does that impact how you view yourself?

The Keepers

Every good fisherman knows that certain fish are attracted to specific baits. Growing up around farm ponds, I quickly learned that a monster channel catfish can hardly resist a juicy piece of awful-smelling stink bait wrapped on a treble hook. Wide-mouth bass love a frisky little minnow. Perch are prone to nightcrawlers, and a Parachute Adams fly is simply too irresistible for a hungry trout.

Fishing takes time and patience, but it also takes skill and effort. Knowing your baits and hooks and mastering your timing separates the fishermen from the "fisherboys." When you're bait fishing, there is a pretty good chance you know what you are going to catch (despite an occasional tree branch or patch of moss).

Fishing with a net is similar to bait fishing but also different in a couple of key ways. Certainly, a lot of casting has to be done, and being at the right place at the right time is crucial. You have to know where to go to get what you want. The biggest difference? If you're successful, you'll pull in not just one but a whole load of slimy fish all at once! And unlike bait fishing, you never know what you're going to catch with a net. The net may be bursting, but true success is measured after the fish are separated—the good from the bad, the big from the small, the keepers from the ones you'll release.

Jesus was a carpenter by trade, but He also knew a thing or two about fishing. He spent a lot of time with fishermen, and He was keenly aware of the challenges they faced. We know of at least one occasion when Jesus saved an otherwise disastrous fishing trip (Luke 5:1–11)!

One day, Jesus used a fishing illustration to make a very important point about heaven. After he finished telling His disciples the parable, Jesus asked them a simple question: *"Do you understand?"* It was as if He was saying, "Don't miss this. It all comes down to this. Yes, I am as patient as any fisherman you will ever meet, but there will come a day when we have to purge the net."

The message was clear: There will be a time when wickedness will no longer be tolerated. Evil will be no more. The catch will be culled: The wicked will be separated from those who have made their peace with God. The Scriptures call those people "righteous," not of their own accord but as a result of having been hooked and netted by the One who calmed the seas. They are the keepers. They have chosen to follow Jesus, and He has made them fishers of men. They have been caught and will never be released!

"Again, the Kingdom of Heaven is like a fishing net that was thrown into the water and caught fish of every kind. When the net was full, they dragged it up onto the shore, sat down, and sorted the good fish into crates, but threw the bad ones away. That is the way it will be at the end of the world. The angels will come and separate the wicked people from the righteous, throwing the wicked into the fiery furnace, where there will be weeping and gnashing of teeth. Do you understand all these things?"

"Yes," they said, "we do."

—Matthew 13:47–51

PAUSE & PONDER:
RECORD YOUR REFLECTIONS AND PERSONAL INSIGHTS

Have you decided to follow Christ? How does knowing that someday good will be separated from evil impact how you live your life today?

DAY 17:

Nailed It

There's a story about a homeowner who suffered from a terribly squeaky floorboard. Try as he might to quiet the annoyance, the problem persisted and nearly drove the man batty. Determined to conquer the pesky squeak, the homeowner hired a carpenter. Within five minutes of his arrival, the carpenter fixed the problem and presented the homeowner with a bill for $1,000.

"How outrageous!" the homeowner protested. "You're charging me $1,000 for less than five minutes of work!"

Calmly, the carpenter asked, "How long had you suffered from the horrible squeak?"

"For more than two years," the homeowner replied. "It was driving me insane!"

"Then surely you will understand that while the nail costs less than a dime, knowing where to drive it was worth $999.90," the carpenter responded. "I have spent a lifetime learning where to properly drive nails. I am happy that today I was able to save you an even more costly trip to a psychiatrist!"

Wisdom applies what is known to what is needed. The best solutions are often derived from a life committed to learning. Unless we first become a student, we will lack the depth of knowledge and experience needed to resolve many of life's issues.

Jesus is the master carpenter. His followers recognize their limitations and look to Him for the insight they need. They are eager to learn from Him. Jesus draws from an ancient storehouse of knowledge that leads us to new insight and understanding, providing much-needed wisdom for the challenges we face today.

> *Then he added, "Every teacher of religious law who becomes a disciple in the Kingdom of Heaven is like a homeowner who brings from his storeroom new gems of truth as well as old."*
> —Matthew 13:52

PAUSE & PONDER:
RECORD YOUR REFLECTIONS AND PERSONAL INSIGHTS

Where do you typically turn when you need an answer? What would it look like to turn to Jesus for the wisdom and knowledge you need?

Sheep, a Shepherd, and a Thief

Of all the comparisons Jesus could have made between man and beast, sheep are His analogy of choice. He doesn't choose lions, tigers, or bears. Instead, Jesus compares us to sheep! So, what do we know about sheep?

One of the first things we learn about sheep is that they thrive in community. Someone may reference a lone wolf but never a lone sheep. Sheep are social creatures by nature. They like to hang out together, but most of all, they have learned there is strength in numbers. Together they stand. Isolated they fall.

Sheep also have impeccable hearing, and they see color. This is helpful given that their only means of defense is to run! It is fair to say they are constantly in tune with their surroundings. If they are to be taken by a predator, it will require a sneak attack.

Sheep instinctively follow, and they are dependent upon their shepherd for survival. While they trust him, they are also demanding of him—when they want food, they want it *now*.

Sheep aren't necessarily stupid, but if they let down their guard, they tend to drift away from the flock. (Not a good idea unless you want to become lamb chops!)

Jesus shares a story that contains three main characters: a flock of sheep, a shepherd, and a thief. Jesus says that the sheep recognize their shepherd's voice—he calls his sheep by name, and wherever he leads, they follow. However, even though the shepherd cares for his flock, Jesus is quick to point out that life as a sheep is not without concern. Unfortunately, there is a thief who comes to steal, kill, and destroy the flock.

It is at this point we begin to easily connect the dots between sheep and people. In the story and in life, there is a thief. He is a deceiver. A masterful impersonator. The ultimate imposter. He sneaks in undercover and waits for the opportune time to strike the sheep that has wandered off. Isolation is his strategy. Fear and terror are his tools. He hopes to separate sheep from the shepherd and the rest of the flock in order to keep them from experiencing the rich, satisfying life the shepherd provides.

Jesus is the Good Shepherd. He constantly tends to His sheep. He calls His sheep by name and deeply desires to care for and nurture them.

Have you heard the Shepherd's voice today? If distance and isolation have hindered your hearing, take notice! The thief may very well be attempting to steal you away, kill your joy, and destroy your life.

Be alert. Be aware. Don't be deceived. Run for the gate! Run before it is too late! Safety and peace reside just inside with the wonderful, caring, and compassionate Good Shepherd.

"I tell you the truth, anyone who sneaks over the wall of a sheepfold, rather than going through the gate, must surely be a thief and a robber! But the one who enters through the gate is the shepherd of the sheep. The gatekeeper opens the gate for him, and the sheep recognize his voice and come to him. He calls his own sheep by name and leads them out. After he has gathered his own flock, he walks ahead of them, and they follow him because they know his voice. They won't follow a stranger; they will run from him because they don't know his voice."

Those who heard Jesus use this illustration didn't understand what he meant, so he explained it to them: "I tell you the truth, I am the gate for the sheep. All who came before me were thieves and robbers. But the true sheep did not listen to them. Yes, I am the gate. Those who come in through me will be saved. They will come and go freely and will find good pastures. The thief's purpose is to steal and kill and destroy. My purpose is to give them a rich and satisfying life.

"I am the good shepherd. The good shepherd sacrifices his life for the sheep. A hired hand will run when he sees a wolf coming. He will abandon the sheep because they don't belong to him and he isn't their shepherd. And so the wolf attacks them and scatters the flock. The hired hand runs away because he's working only for the money and doesn't really care about the sheep.

"I am the good shepherd; I know my own sheep, and they know me, just as my Father knows me and I know the Father. So I sacrifice my life for the sheep. I have other sheep, too, that are not in this sheepfold. I must bring them also. They will listen to my voice, and there will be one flock with one shepherd."

—John 10:1–16

PAUSE & PONDER:
RECORD YOUR REFLECTIONS AND PERSONAL INSIGHTS

Where have you seen the thief—the master impersonator—stealing and destroying your life? What does this parable teach us about ourselves? What does it teach us about God?

Come Home

The sheep business is a fragile enterprise. Sheep can easily get lost, and they are extremely vulnerable creatures. They are in constant need of leadership, provision, and protection.

If a shepherd discovers that one of his sheep has wandered from the flock, he will do his best to rescue the lost sheep so long as he does not neglect the security of the rest of his flock. While the lost sheep is certainly a distraction, the shepherd is determined to keep his flock whole.

Like sheep, we are prone to wander and easily led astray. We are in constant need of leadership, provision, and protection.

The good news is that our Good Shepherd will come searching for us when we are AWOL (absent without leave). He doesn't distinguish between a wanderer, a traitor, or a deserter. His love for us compels Him to risk it all to find the one.

While God is deeply committed to us, He is not foolish. He won't beg us or drag us back to the flock. He will not force

His way. No, He knows that His sheep recognize His still, small voice—that gentle whisper that summons them home. As much as He hates to, He will eventually turn us over to our own ways. He loves us so much that He leaves it up to us. Will we come home, or will we continue to wander?

Where are you today? The Good Shepherd has you on His mind. Whether you are in the flock or have run amuck, He longs to be with you, lead you, provide for you, and protect you from all harm. Listen for His voice. Softly and tenderly, He beckons, "Come home."

> *"If a man has a hundred sheep and one of them wanders away, what will he do? Won't he leave the ninety-nine others on the hills and go out to search for the one that is lost? And if he finds it, I tell you the truth, he will rejoice over it more than over the ninety-nine that didn't wander away! In the same way, it is not my heavenly Father's will that even one of these little ones should perish."*
> —Matthew 18:12–14

PAUSE & PONDER:
RECORD YOUR REFLECTIONS AND PERSONAL INSIGHTS

Where are you today? If you've wandered from the flock, what would it look like to listen to God's voice calling you home?

When Duty Calls

Serving others is hard work. Just about the time we think we have plowed through another day, we remember it's time to eat and somebody—as in us—has to fry up dinner in a pan. And then, of course, there are always the dishes! Serving is exhausting, but serving is also an opportunity to love.

The greatest leaders are known for their service. What's more, the best leaders serve out of love and without expecting recognition. They aren't looking over their shoulders expecting someone to pin a medal on their aprons. True leaders serve out of a sense of duty, understanding that service is simply what they are called to do.

Rather than pouting as we wait for people to cheer in the presence of our grandeur, we should look for what needs to be done, take initiative, and continue in our service. When we serve without expecting accolades, it is a sure sign that we have matured as leaders—we are no longer serving from our heads but from our hearts.

In our willingness to sacrifice for others, we must remember that, ultimately, we don't serve people. Rather, we are in the service of His Majesty the King. Serving is not what we do; it is who we are: We are servants of our Lord. We have simply answered the call and fulfilled our duty.

> *"When a servant comes in from plowing or taking care of sheep, does his master say, 'Come in and eat with me'? No, he says, 'Prepare my meal, put on your apron, and serve me while I eat. Then you can eat later.' And does the master thank the servant for doing what he was told to do? Of course not. In the same way, when you obey me you should say, 'We are unworthy servants who have simply done our duty.'"*
>
> —Luke 17:7–10

PAUSE & PONDER:
RECORD YOUR REFLECTIONS AND PERSONAL INSIGHTS

Have you considered how important your duty to serve is? How have you answered the call?

DAY 21:

Believing in You

W ho are they? Who are the people you could never repay no matter how hard you tried? Is it a parent, a teacher, a friend, a neighbor, a relative, or perhaps an absolute stranger? Whoever it is and whenever it was, you will never forget the love of the people who believed in you.

The debt you owe these people reaches far beyond financial means. Maybe they devoted every minute of every day to loving you and seeing you through. But regardless of how long they were in your life, they gave you a great gift. Their motivation wasn't rooted in obligation, the need for control, or the hope of some sort of return on their investment. Instead, their compelling generosity came from a love so deep that they would have paid whatever the price to ransom your future.

Why did they do it? Because to them, you were worth it. Not because you earned it, deserved it, or promised to pay them back. No, this kind of love and commitment came from a deep admiration for you and all that you could become. This love saw potential and laid it all on the line because they believed. Believed in what? In you.

They believed that you would carry the banner of love and generosity into the lives of those you have the power to influence.

You've been given an example to follow, and now the choice is yours to make: Will you give or take? Bless or curse? Love or hate?

The only way to repay a debt of gratitude is with our lives. Decide today to make yours count. Pay it forward with the love you have received. Give generously from a heart that was made full by the love of other people and, most of all, by the One who is Love and always believes in you.

"Therefore, the Kingdom of Heaven can be compared to a king who decided to bring his accounts up to date with servants who had borrowed money from him. In the process, one of his debtors was brought in who owed him millions of dollars. He couldn't pay, so his master ordered that he be sold—along with his wife, his children, and everything he owned—to pay the debt.

"But the man fell down before his master and begged him, 'Please, be patient with me, and I will pay it all.' Then his master was filled with pity for him, and he released him and forgave his debt.

"But when the man left the king, he went to a fellow servant who owed him a few thousand dollars. He grabbed him by the throat and demanded instant payment.

"His fellow servant fell down before him and begged for a little more time. 'Be patient with me, and I will pay it,' he pleaded. But his creditor wouldn't wait. He had the man arrested and put in prison until the debt could be paid in full.

"When some of the other servants saw this, they were very upset. They went to the king and told him everything that had happened. Then the king called in the man he had forgiven and said, 'You evil servant! I forgave you that tremendous debt because you pleaded with me. Shouldn't you have mercy on your fellow servant, just as I had mercy on you?' Then the angry king sent the man to prison to be tortured until he had paid his entire debt.

"That's what my heavenly Father will do to you if you refuse to forgive your brothers and sisters from your heart."

—Matthew 18:23–35

PAUSE & PONDER:
RECORD YOUR REFLECTIONS AND PERSONAL INSIGHTS

Name one person who believed in you and invested in you. How did they impact your life? How can you pay it forward?

DAY 22:

Ours to Render

Jesus tells a story about a good guy who is attacked by some bad fellows. In terrible shape and left for dead, the man is ultimately saved by the good deeds of an unlikely stranger. Several travelers see the man in need but for whatever reason, justified or not, they choose to keep walking and ignore the opportunity to help someone in a desperate situation.

Why do they move on? Are they indifferent? Do they lack the resources or the competency to lend a hand? Are they too busy to get involved? We are left to wonder. Whatever their reasons, the wounded man's plight confirms something we all wrestle with: Bad things happen to good people for no apparent rhyme or reason.

When bad things happen to bad people, we tend to think they got what they deserved. But when bad things happen to good people, we are confused and even indignant. One would think some level of favor or protection would surround those who are committed to doing good (or at the very least, those who aren't looking to hurt anyone else). But such is not the case. Bad things happen with no regard to our personal goodness.

If we pause and think it through, we should be disgusted in either case. Bad is bad whether it falls on the just or unjust. Bad things are no worse when they fall on good people and no better when they fall on the worst. And seeing bad things in the world should make us mad—mad enough that we, with God's help, do our best to rectify a wrong regardless of the victim's moral track record.

We find a glimpse of Jesus's heart when He encourages us to love our enemies. We are called to love without weighing a person's righteousness or considering the pain they may have caused. In essence, we are called to love the sinner but hate the sin.

The challenge presented is simple but, at times, extremely difficult to do: love. No more, no less. Love is to be our only response and our only responsibility. Love with no regard to race, ethnicity, orientation, beliefs, or actions. Love is supreme. It is the key to overcoming evil with good on any road we travel.

Bad things happen. Good things do too. The opportunity to love depends on me, and it depends on you. Love can be tough, and love can be tender. Either way it is ours to render.

> *Jesus replied with a story: "A Jewish man was traveling from Jerusalem down to Jericho, and he was attacked by bandits. They stripped him of his clothes, beat him up, and left him half dead beside the road.*

"By chance a priest came along. But when he saw the man lying there, he crossed to the other side of the road and passed him by. A Temple assistant walked over and looked at him lying there, but he also passed by on the other side.

"Then a despised Samaritan came along, and when he saw the man, he felt compassion for him. Going over to him, the Samaritan soothed his wounds with olive oil and wine and bandaged them. Then he put the man on his own donkey and took him to an inn, where he took care of him. The next day he handed the innkeeper two silver coins, telling him, 'Take care of this man. If his bill runs higher than this, I'll pay you the next time I'm here.'

"Now which of these three would you say was a neighbor to the man who was attacked by bandits?" Jesus asked.

The man replied, "The one who showed him mercy."

Then Jesus said, "Yes, now go and do the same."
—Luke 10:30–37

PAUSE & PONDER:
RECORD YOUR REFLECTIONS AND PERSONAL INSIGHTS

Do you tend to think that some people are more deserving of help than others? Ask God for an opportunity to love someone who is typically hard for you to love.

A Tale of Three Friends

Jesus tells a story about the challenges and impact of genuine friendship. We are introduced to three friends entangled in a test certain to challenge the best of relationships.

Imagine being awakened in the middle of the night by a friend looking for milk and cookies, a warm bed, and a bedtime story. It would be one thing if the house was on fire, but rattling the gate for a midnight snack? Who does that? An *intruding* friend does that. We have all had friends like these, friends who show up out of nowhere expecting the royal treatment. They are never more your friend than when they need something from you. As they say, "A friend in need is a friend indeed!"

What about the person who wakes up a friend in the middle of the night begging on behalf of another friend who showed up unannounced? Who does that? An *imposing* friend. We have all been there too. Sometimes, our needs exceed our ability, so what do we do? We transfer our burden onto the backs of those we love. We get by with a little help from our friends!

What kind of friend rolls out of bed (albeit somewhat reluctantly) to help a friend *help a friend*, even if that friend lacks common decency? An *intentional* friend. The request is inconvenient, annoying, and intrusive, but that is what friends do. They look out for each other.

A true friend is a friend at all times—someone who gives the benefit of the doubt and assumes there must be a good reason for what appears to be unfriendly behavior. No wonder a good friend has been described as someone who walks in when the rest of the world walks out. Friends are in it together. Great friends have your back, and they intentionally look for opportunities to return the favor. Midnight seems to be as good of a time as any!

God must feel like the friend pulling back the covers and handing out snacks in the middle of the night. He is the friend who never sleeps. We come pounding on His door and demanding what we want, and what is His response? Basically, "Thanks for stopping by. It's good to see you. You have not because you ask not. I love you, and I am here for you, even in the middle of the night."

He is truly our friend despite our selfish motives. Even when we come to Him thinking only of what we want and not looking to connect with Him, He will still be there for us. He will still provide. Because that's who He is—a friend like no other. A friend who, despite our selfishness, loves us and does what He can to lighten our load, even if it means providing a cozy bed and a fresh loaf of bread under the light of the moon. That's friendship. That's our friend Jesus. He is in it with us for the long haul.

Then, teaching them more about prayer, he used this story: "Suppose you went to a friend's house at midnight, wanting to borrow three loaves of bread. You say to him, 'A friend of mine has just arrived for a visit, and I have nothing for him to eat.' And suppose he calls out from his bedroom, 'Don't bother me. The door is locked for the night, and my family and I are all in bed. I can't help you.' But I tell you this—though he won't do it for friendship's sake, if you keep knocking long enough, he will get up and give you whatever you need because of your shameless persistence.

"And so I tell you, keep on asking, and you will receive what you ask for. Keep on seeking, and you will find. Keep on knocking, and the door will be opened to you. For everyone who asks, receives. Everyone who seeks, finds. And to everyone who knocks, the door will be opened.

"You fathers—if your children ask for a fish, do you give them a snake instead? Or if they ask for an egg, do you give them a scorpion? Of course not! So if you sinful people know how to give good gifts to your children, how much more will your heavenly Father give the Holy Spirit to those who ask him."

—Luke 11:5–13

PAUSE & PONDER:
RECORD YOUR REFLECTIONS AND PERSONAL INSIGHTS

Who are the friends you can count on in the middle of the night? Are you a friend who can be counted on? Do you think of Jesus as a friend like that?

DAY 24:

Party Hardy

J esus liked to party. He loved people and loved being with them. Jesus was fascinated by people, and He was a student of human behavior. He was the ultimate "people watcher." So much so that He even noted how people clamored for the good seats at private parties.

People are predictable. Humans tend to posture and position themselves for opportunities that will set them up nicely for power, prestige, and plenty of press. "Look at me! Look who I'm with. See where I'm sitting. I bet you wish you were here!" SELFIE!!

People become so self-conscious and so self-absorbed that they often forget to be present, or they pretend to be who they think others want them to be rather than who they really are. See and be seen is the goal. "I'm in! I'm connected! I'm cool! Like my outfit? Did you see the car I drove up in? I'm glad you are here so long as you don't take my spot in the limelight."

Jesus has different perspective. Rather than focus on the invite and the just-right seat, why not be the one doing the inviting? And while you're at it, why not shake up the guest list a bit?

Jesus encourages us to put some ragamuffins on the list. Include some down-and-outers, not just a bunch of up-and-comers and upper-crust elites. Invite some crumbs! Go for it! Throw a party with a group of people who have nothing in common and nothing to offer in return, not even a bag of ice.

Surrounding yourself with a posse of people just like yourself is like reading the same story for the tenth time in a row—it's a slow train to boredom. The key to a fun and memorable party is the art of conversation and the stories that accompany the people who walk through the door.

So, mix it up! Party hardy! Dare to step out of your comfort zone and invite some interesting—no, some *really* interesting—characters to your next gathering.

Try it and see. Like Jesus, take some time to notice and study human behavior. You will likely discover that no one cares who is sitting next to whom. Not even you! Why? Because they will be having too much fun getting to know people and making new friends, all because of you!

When Jesus noticed that all who had come to the dinner were trying to sit in the seats of honor near the head of the table, he gave them this advice: "When you are invited to a wedding feast, don't sit in the seat of honor. What if someone who is more distinguished than you has also been invited? The host will come and say, 'Give this person your seat.' Then you will be embarrassed, and you will have to take whatever seat is left at the foot of the table! "Instead, take the lowest place at the foot of the table. Then when your host sees you, he will come and say, 'Friend, we have a better place for you!' Then you will be honored in front of all the other guests. For those who exalt themselves will be humbled, and those who humble themselves will be exalted."

Then he turned to his host. "When you put on a luncheon or a banquet," he said, "don't invite your friends, brothers, relatives, and rich neighbors. For they will invite you back, and that will be your only reward. Instead, invite the poor, the crippled, the lame, and the blind. Then at the resurrection of the righteous, God will reward you for inviting those who could not repay you."'

—Luke 14:7–14

PAUSE & PONDER:
RECORD YOUR REFLECTIONS AND PERSONAL INSIGHTS

Whose opinions tend to matter the most to you? Who do you find yourself trying to impress? How can you become more hospitable to people who are different from you?

Excuse Me

Jesus tells a story about a man who spared no expense to throw an extravagant and elaborate party for his friends, but sadly the RSVPs were few. How was that possible? Why would anyone turn down such a great opportunity for so much fun?

It's simple. It wasn't the food, it wasn't the location, it wasn't the cost, and it wasn't the company. It simply came down to excuses.

"Sorry, I wish I could, but I can't." "If I had only known sooner." "I'm buried right now." "I forgot." "I need to feed my goldfish." Or the grade school classic, "My dog ate it!"

Certainly, there are times when circumstances are out of our control. An unforeseen interruption, accident, or change in events alters our course. But most of the time, let's face it—we do what we want to do. We have other things in mind, and we'd just rather not. What benefits us most and requires the least amount of effort is what gets done. We would rather make excuses than make priorities.

We are masters of the put-off, the letdown, the good intentions, and the would've, could've, or should've. The "Sorry I'm late" or "Let's try again soon." And the good ole standby: "Maybe next time."

Let's be honest. Let's quit making excuses and come clean: We've got better things to do. Or do we? If we dig a little deeper, we may find that our excuses are rooted in the flawed belief that relationships take too much effort and time. People are messy, and conversations just go on and on.

Jesus never made excuses. He made room. He made exceptions. He made a way. He lived a life of interruptions and made time for what really mattered. Walk-ins were welcome. He built margin into His day for people. People were His priority— so much so that it cost Him His life.

What do you say? How about we cut back on the lame excuses and the good intentions and start showing up, being present, and making others a priority in our lives.

The bottom-line? Less of us and more of Him results in fewer excuses and more opportunities to love. We can make excuses, or we can make a way.

> *Jesus replied with this story: "A man prepared a great feast and sent out many invitations. When the banquet was ready, he sent his servant to tell the guests, 'Come, the banquet is ready.' But they all began making excuses. One said, 'I have just bought a field and must inspect it. Please excuse me.' Another said, 'I have just bought five pairs of oxen, and I want to try them out. Please excuse me.' Another said, 'I just got married, so I can't come.'*

"The servant returned and told his master what they had said. His master was furious and said, 'Go quickly into the streets and alleys of the town and invite the poor, the crippled, the blind, and the lame.' After the servant had done this, he reported, 'There is still room for more.' So his master said, 'Go out into the country lanes and behind the hedges and urge anyone you find to come, so that the house will be full. For none of those I first invited will get even the smallest taste of my banquet.'"

—Luke 14:16–24

PAUSE & PONDER:
RECORD YOUR REFLECTIONS AND PERSONAL INSIGHTS

Do you tend to see people as a priority or an interruption? How can you create more margin in your life for building relationships?

Count the Cost

Anything worth having comes at a cost. There is no such thing as a free lunch—it may not have cost you a dime, but it cost somebody something. Counting the cost of an endeavor is not something we should consider after the fact; it's where we must begin.

We'll only find success when we begin with the end in mind, so we should make every effort to know what we are getting into. A wise king does not go to battle without first assessing whether his troops have the strength to win. Without counting the cost upfront, disaster and defeat await us.

Being a disciple of Jesus is not a walk in the park but rather a march into battle where the enemy is a strong and experienced warrior. We should expect a fight. But we should also expect to win. Our enemy comes to steal, kill, and destroy, but he is not God's equal. He is a mere angel with a God complex. If God is with us, who could ever defeat us?

Jesus's offer of salvation is a gift available for the taking, but one thing is for sure: It was not without cost. Jesus's victory came at a price. It was far from free.

The soldier who has counted the cost will not be lost in battle. He will prevail. Though it may require sacrifice, pain, and unwavering commitment, the soldier of the cross will win in the end by giving Jesus his all. As missionary Jim Elliot so eloquently conveyed, "He is no fool who gives what he cannot keep to gain what he cannot lose."

> *"But don't begin until you count the cost. For who would begin construction of a building without first calculating the cost to see if there is enough money to finish it? Otherwise, you might complete only the foundation before running out of money, and then everyone would laugh at you. They would say, 'There's the person who started that building and couldn't afford to finish it!'*

> *"Or what king would go to war against another king without first sitting down with his counselors to discuss whether his army of 10,000 could defeat the 20,000 soldiers marching against him? And if he can't, he will send a delegation to discuss terms of peace while the enemy is still far away. So you cannot become my disciple without giving up everything you own."*
>
> —Luke 14:28–33

PAUSE & PONDER:
RECORD YOUR REFLECTIONS AND PERSONAL INSIGHTS

Do you agree with this statement: Anything worth having comes at a cost? Why or why not?

DAY 27:

Regain and Retain

W hat do you value? Time? Money? Peace? Family? Friends? Possessions? Integrity? Toys? Fitness? Fun? Opinions? Status? What makes those things valuable to you?

Some things are very expensive but prove useless in the wrong hands, like a pricey tool you've never learned how to use. Other things are inexpensive but priceless to the one who owns them. For example, who hasn't moved heaven and earth to lay hands on a remote control or a set of car keys? These relatively inexpensive items are often highly valued and can cause great anxiety when they are missing. Not only is the possession misplaced, but our peace is also lost. Both have value.

Some things have monetary value, while others have emotional value. And yet we tend to think of *valuables* as being things that are easily quantifiable. But what about the things that are harder to measure, like love, stability, harmony, a moral compass, a good attitude, or our health? These too have value. If we aren't careful, we won't realize what we have until it's gone. A good marriage, strong friendships, or even an intimate walk with God can be gone before we know it.

Maybe today is a great opportunity to hit the pause button and take inventory of what you really value. What would you miss if it was gone? What can you do to safeguard the role those "valuables" play in your life?

Is there something of value that has quietly vanished from your life? Perhaps you took it for granted and failed to notice it had slipped away. It is not too late to try to find it. Go after it. If it is truly of value, it will be worth the effort. Do all you can to regain and retain it!

> *"Or suppose a woman has ten silver coins and loses one. Won't she light a lamp and sweep the entire house and search carefully until she finds it? And when she finds it, she will call in her friends and neighbors and say, 'Rejoice with me because I have found my lost coin.' In the same way, there is joy in the presence of God's angels when even one sinner repents."*
>
> — Luke 15:8–10

PAUSE & PONDER:
RECORD YOUR REFLECTIONS AND PERSONAL INSIGHTS

Have you lost something you once greatly valued? How did that loss make you feel? To what extent would you go to regain the lost valuable?

Time to Party

We live in an age of instant gratification. While there is no harm per se in an instant reward, many things take time to develop to their fullest potential. As the saying goes: "Rome wasn't built in a day."

The prodigal son from Jesus's parable got too far ahead of himself. His desire for instant gratification left him empty-handed. He failed to realize that in life you have a choice: pay now or pay later. He rocketed into the high life but landed in the mud. On the brink of starvation, he finally comes to his senses and makes his way home.

No doubt the prodigal son suffered loss, but he never escaped the unconditional love of his father. Despite having truly blown it, he is greeted with forgiveness and compassion from his father. He was fortunate—not everyone lands in a safety net when they jump. We can learn from the prodigal son's experience without having to live out his missteps in our own lives.

Perhaps the most beautiful lesson in this parable is seen in the heart of the father. When his son comes home, the father decides life is too short to wallow in the mistakes of the past. He chooses to forgive his son, and he throws a party to celebrate his return.

However, that's not how everyone sees it. Rather than celebrating his brother's return, the older brother becomes angry and resentful. He refuses to go to the party and confronts his father about how unfair the whole situation is—after all, he had been working hard while his younger brother wasted his inheritance. The older brother's angst is something many of us can relate to. Who doesn't want to be rewarded for doing the "right" thing?

The father demonstrates deep, unconditional love toward his older son as well. He encourages him not to miss what matters most, and he invites him into the celebration. The father's response is one we can learn from: When good things happen, slay the fattened calf! The lost has been found. The wanderer has made his way home. It's time to party! Commemorate the good times because dark, rainy days are sure to come. As for now, have mercy, extend grace, and take a minute to celebrate *the* Son.

We need to lighten up and be less critical of others and ourselves. Our role is not to judge but to forgive and to love at all times. Yes, at *all* times, even when it's hard. Even when people repeatedly make bad choices. In so doing, we will love as we have been loved—with a love that's born in an instant but grows throughout eternity.

To illustrate the point further, Jesus told them this story: "A man had two sons. The younger son told his father, 'I want my share of your estate now before you die.' So his father agreed to divide his wealth between his sons.

"A few days later this younger son packed all his belongings and moved to a distant land, and there he wasted all his money in wild living. About the time his money ran out, a great famine swept over the land, and he began to starve. He persuaded a local farmer to hire him, and the man sent him into his fields to feed the pigs. The young man became so hungry that even the pods he was feeding the pigs looked good to him. But no one gave him anything.

"When he finally came to his senses, he said to himself, 'At home even the hired servants have food enough to spare, and here I am dying of hunger! I will go home to my father and say, "Father, I have sinned against both heaven and you, and I am no longer worthy of being called your son. Please take me on as a hired servant."'

"So he returned home to his father. And while he was still a long way off, his father saw him coming. Filled with love and compassion, he ran to his son, embraced him, and kissed him. His son said to him, 'Father, I have sinned against both heaven and you, and I am no longer worthy of being called your son.'

"But his father said to the servants, 'Quick! Bring the finest robe in the house and put it on him. Get a ring for his finger and sandals for his feet. And kill the calf we have been fattening. We must celebrate with a feast, for this son of mine was dead and has now returned to life. He was lost, but now he is found.' So the party began.

"Meanwhile, the older son was in the fields working. When he returned home, he heard music and dancing in the house, and he asked one of the servants what was going on. 'Your brother is back,' he was told, 'and your father has killed the fattened calf. We are celebrating because of his safe return.'

"The older brother was angry and wouldn't go in. His father came out and begged him, but he replied, 'All these years I've slaved for you and never once refused to do a single thing you told me to. And in all that time you never gave me even one young goat for a feast with my friends. Yet when this son of yours comes back after squandering your money on prostitutes, you celebrate by killing the fattened calf!'

"His father said to him, 'Look, dear son, you have always stayed by me, and everything I have is yours. We had to celebrate this happy day. For your brother was dead and has come back to life! He was lost, but now he is found!'"

—Luke 15:11–32

PAUSE & PONDER:
RECORD YOUR REFLECTIONS AND PERSONAL INSIGHTS

Do you know someone who has truly (maybe repeatedly) blown it? How can you be less like the older brother and more like the father in the way you treat that person?

DAY 29:

Loosen Your Grip

Jesus tells a story of a dishonest rascal who is caught mismanaging the money of his wealthy employer. When the employer realizes what the manager is doing, he confronts and fires him. At first glance, it seems like cutting our losses and moving on might be the moral of the story. But then the manager does something unexpected.

Realizing he can't save his job, he decides he might as well save his friendships. He cuts deals with his employer's debtors, getting some of his employer's money back and earning himself favor with his friends in the process.

The rich man had evidently made up his mind that he would never see his money again, so when he hears that the shrewd manager has found a way to get back at least part of his money, he is quite pleased. The dishonest manager may have been in a pickle, but he is anything but stupid—he knows that debtors love deep discounts and that his boss would be happy to retain something when nothing was his only option. He turns fraud into friendship!

Interestingly enough, the story is not about the ten best ways to dupe your boss or how to buy friends cheaper by the dozen. From Jesus's perspective, the lesson is ultimately about the power of generosity. Without question, the manager is a bad employee, but even his bad example can be used for good. Jesus is quick to point out the benefits of using whatever resources we have to help others and make friends in the process.

It is easy to spend another person's money, but when it comes to letting go of our own stack of bills, we tend to have a much tighter grip. You might be thinking, "But I've worked hard for what I have. Am I just supposed to throw it away trying to get people to like me?" Hardly! Jesus never suggested that we waste our money or allow ourselves to be taken advantage of. We are called to be shrewd stewards of the blessings God provides. But at the same time, Jesus advocates for openhandedness. He assures us that generosity is a great investment, one that stores up lasting treasures in heaven while also doing a world of good today.

When we think about generosity, we tend to think about money. And while giving financially is certainly a great way to demonstrate a benevolent heart, it is not the only way. There are many ways to be generous with our resources. We can also give of our time, talents, words, praise, mercy, grace, and love, to name a few.

Generosity places a high value on relationships, and Jesus knew what He was doing when He encouraged us to use our resources to make friends. Helping others pays great dividends.

When we give a little, we gain a lot. No wonder Jesus says it is more blessed to give than to receive. When we loosen our grip, we reap the reward. If we hold on too tightly, we squeeze the life out of what we've got.

Jesus told this story to his disciples: "There was a certain rich man who had a manager handling his affairs. One day a report came that the manager was wasting his employer's money. So the employer called him in and said, 'What's this I hear about you? Get your report in order, because you are going to be fired.'

"The manager thought to himself, 'Now what? My boss has fired me. I don't have the strength to dig ditches, and I'm too proud to beg. Ah, I know how to ensure that I'll have plenty of friends who will give me a home when I am fired.'

"So he invited each person who owed money to his employer to come and discuss the situation. He asked the first one, 'How much do you owe him?' The man replied, 'I owe him 800 gallons of olive oil.' So the manager told him, 'Take the bill and quickly change it to 400 gallons.'

"'And how much do you owe my employer?' he asked the next man. 'I owe him 1,000 bushels of wheat,' was the reply. 'Here,' the manager said, 'take the bill and change it to 800 bushels.'

"The rich man had to admire the dishonest rascal for being so shrewd. And it is true that the children of this world are more shrewd in dealing with the world around them than are the children of the light. Here's the lesson: Use your worldly resources to benefit others and make friends. Then, when your possessions are gone, they will welcome you to an eternal home."

—Luke 16:1–9

PAUSE & PONDER:
RECORD YOUR REFLECTIONS AND PERSONAL INSIGHTS

Where is God asking you to be more generous? Is it with your money, time, energy, encouragement, or something else? Ask God to help you loosen your grip on that thing.

Carried or Buried?

Let's be honest, compared to most of the world, many of us possess nearly everything life has to offer. We enjoy creature comforts that others only dream of. Sure, we have challenges and disappointments but, on the grand scale, life didn't throw us lemons—it lobbed us powder puffs. We are somehow among the privileged.

Should we feel guilty about that? I don't think so. But we need to realize how blessed we are and find tangible ways to make the world a better place. We are wrong to look the other way. The key is to recognize the blessings we have and to seek ways to raise the quality of life for everyone. What can we do to contribute to the livelihood and well-being of our fellow man?

Privilege alone doesn't guarantee success. Oftentimes, those who appear to have it all together are the ones who are falling apart, while those who look like they have little to offer tend to understand life's secrets of contentment. Our choices matter, and we all benefit or suffer from the decisions we make in life. The paths we choose will determine whether we are carried to the other side or buried and left behind with all our stuff.

In the end, life is not about gaining all you can get; it's about giving all you've got. As we navigate our day-to-day lives, it is important to remember that it profits a man little if he gains the world yet loses his soul (Mark 8:36).

Relationships are the only transportable treasures from this life, not the trinkets that catch our eyes but fade with time. Decide today to do what you can to take some folks with you.

Jesus said, "There was a certain rich man who was splendidly clothed in purple and fine linen and who lived each day in luxury. At his gate lay a poor man named Lazarus who was covered with sores. As Lazarus lay there longing for scraps from the rich man's table, the dogs would come and lick his open sores.

"Finally, the poor man died and was carried by the angels to sit beside Abraham at the heavenly banquet. The rich man also died and was buried, and he went to the place of the dead. There, in torment, he saw Abraham in the far distance with Lazarus at his side.

"The rich man shouted, 'Father Abraham, have some pity! Send Lazarus over here to dip the tip of his finger in water and cool my tongue. I am in anguish in these flames.'

"But Abraham said to him, 'Son, remember that during your lifetime you had everything you wanted, and Lazarus had nothing. So now he is here being comforted, and you are in anguish. And besides, there is a great chasm separating us. No one can cross over to you from here, and no one can cross over to us from there.'

"Then the rich man said, 'Please, Father Abraham, at least send him to my father's home. For I have five brothers, and I want him to warn them so they don't end up in this place of torment.'

"But Abraham said, 'Moses and the prophets have warned them. Your brothers can read what they wrote.'

"The rich man replied, 'No, Father Abraham! But if someone is sent to them from the dead, then they will repent of their sins and turn to God.'

"But Abraham said, 'If they won't listen to Moses and the prophets, they won't be persuaded even if someone rises from the dead.'"

—Luke 16:19–31

PAUSE & PONDER:
RECORD YOUR REFLECTIONS AND PERSONAL INSIGHTS

How can you use what you've been given to improve someone else's life? Who are you bringing with you as you follow Jesus?

DAY 31:

The Time is Now

Success is rarely achieved based solely on the time we put into something. Success has a lot to do with timing. You are probably familiar with the expression, "He was just at the right place at the right time." Being at the right place at the right time has proven effective time and time again. However, more than simply the time invested or perfect timing, success comes to those who are prepared to make the most of an opportunity.

Jesus tells a story about a landowner who hires people to work in his vineyard at different times throughout the day. At the end of the day, the landowner pays the laborers who only worked an hour the same amount as those who had worked all day long. At first glance, it seems incredibly unfair. You can likely relate to that feeling. We all know someone who has paid their dues but didn't get what they wanted or others who seem to succeed by no means of their own. It sure sounds like luck played a significant role in their outcome.

Success depends on many factors. There is no guarantee that putting in more time will equal more success, and there is no guarantee that we will be at the right place at the right time. But one thing is for sure: If we aren't prepared—if we aren't expecting and looking for an opportunity to come our way— then we are very likely to miss it. In Jesus's story, those who are looking and waiting for work are the workers who are ready to go when the landowner hires them. When preparedness meets opportunity, great things fall in line.

Rather than complain and compare ourselves to the overachievers, the so-called "silver spooners," and lucky ducks, we should commit ourselves to being ready for what God has for us. If we don't know what we are looking for, we are likely to miss it, so our first step is to clarify what it is we want. Next, we need to ask the Lord to open our eyes and help us see opportunities like we've never seen them before.

Most of all, let us remember that on this highway called life, we spend a whole lot more time on the road than we do visiting our favorite sites. We might as well enjoy the ride. If we aren't careful, the effort we put in to trying to "succeed" might not be worth the struggle.

When we live a little every day, we get a lot out of life. We can't wait for perfect timing or just hope to be in the right place at the right time. We must be prepared. The time is now to live our lives and seize the day along the way!

"For the Kingdom of Heaven is like the landowner
who went out early one morning to hire workers for

his vineyard. He agreed to pay the normal daily wage and sent them out to work.

"At nine o'clock in the morning he was passing through the marketplace and saw some people standing around doing nothing. So he hired them, telling them he would pay them whatever was right at the end of the day. So they went to work in the vineyard. At noon and again at three o'clock he did the same thing.

"At five o'clock that afternoon he was in town again and saw some more people standing around. He asked them, 'Why haven't you been working today?'

"They replied, 'Because no one hired us.'

"The landowner told them, 'Then go out and join the others in my vineyard.'

"That evening he told the foreman to call the workers in and pay them, beginning with the last workers first. When those hired at five o'clock were paid, each received a full day's wage. When those hired first came to get their pay, they assumed they would receive more. But they, too, were paid a day's wage. When they received their pay, they protested to the owner, 'Those people worked only one hour, and yet you've paid them just as much as you paid us who worked all day in the scorching heat.'

"He answered one of them, 'Friend, I haven't been unfair! Didn't you agree to work all day for the usual wage? Take your money and go. I wanted to pay this last worker the same as you. Is it against the law for me to do what I want with my money? Should you be jealous because I am kind to others?'

"So those who are last now will be first then, and those who are first will be last."

—Matthew 20:1–16

PAUSE & PONDER:
RECORD YOUR REFLECTIONS AND PERSONAL INSIGHTS

What factors do you think lead to success? What's one step you could take to be more prepared when an opportunity comes your way?

Two Ears and One Mouth

When it comes to prayer, many of us only visit God occasionally, often at set times and places. Maybe you pray before meals, on Sunday mornings, or when you're really in a bind. But there are some people who have found a less formal, more relaxed way of connecting with God. They simply converse with him along life's way. They have learned that God doesn't require appointments: With Him, walk-ins are always welcomed!

Jesus challenges us to pray constantly. How is this possible? The key is realizing that prayer is an attitude and a mindset more than something that has to be done at a specific time or place. Whether on our knees or on our feet, conversing with our heavenly Father can become a way of life.

Prayer is a dialogue not a monologue. We tend to think we have to do most of the talking, but we would do well to talk less and listen more. We were, in fact, given two ears and one mouth. This ratio is a good indicator of the role we might play in prayer. Listening twice as much as we speak is an idea worth considering.

Try it. Be still and observe what He has to say throughout the day, for surely, He is communicating with us on multiple levels. Whether through His Word, a song, a devotion, a little child, an elderly relative, a scene from nature, or the pit of pain and suffering, He is there, constantly breathing life and love into every minute of every day. He doesn't yell. He whispers in a still, small voice. If we aren't listening, we just might miss it!

Stay tuned. Stay connected and plugged in. Look for God's presence in your life. He is there. "Remain in the vine," as Jesus would say. Seek to do life with Jesus by walking with Him and talking with Him in a constant attitude of prayer. You've got His ear. Does He have yours?

> *"There was a judge in a certain city," he said, "who neither feared God nor cared about people. A widow of that city came to him repeatedly, saying, 'Give me justice in this dispute with my enemy.' The judge ignored her for a while, but finally he said to himself, 'I don't fear God or care about people, but this woman is driving me crazy. I'm going to see that she gets justice, because she is wearing me out with her constant requests!'"*
>
> *Then the Lord said, "Learn a lesson from this unjust judge. Even he rendered a just decision in the end. So don't you think God will surely give justice to*

his chosen people who cry out to him day and night? Will he keep putting them off? I tell you, he will grant justice to them quickly! But when the Son of Man returns, how many will he find on the earth who have faith?"

—Luke 18:2–8

PAUSE & PONDER:
RECORD YOUR REFLECTIONS AND PERSONAL INSIGHTS

When you pray, do you tend to do more talking or listening? How would adopting a mindset of constant prayer impact your daily life?

DAY 33:

Embrace Humility

Self-confidence is good. A lack of confidence is a waste of potential. We all have a friend who has an incredible gift but is too hesitant to share it with a larger group of people. Maybe your friend is someone who can turn any party into a blast but can't quite muster enough courage to share their brilliance at an impromptu talent show.

However, being overly confident leads to pride, and pride, well, it's the last step before the fall. As the old saying goes, "The bigger they are, the harder they fall." God is not big on pride. As his followers, we are called to embrace humility to the point that it becomes second nature.

Jesus says that the proud will be humbled, but the humble will be honored. He doesn't say the proud *might* be humbled. He says they *will be*. Pride leads to humiliation. Humility leads to honor. If we are not careful, a desire for the limelight can make our souls sick.

Everyone has the potential to either feed their pride or practice humility. One leads to separation—creating distance in relationships—while the other leads to a life of connection and service.

A famous mountain climber agreed to take a photo with a group of hikers before they made their way to the summit. As the group posed for the photo, a young climber interrupted and corrected the famous climber's handling of an ice axe. Without hesitation, the expert smiled, made the adjustment, and thanked the young climber. The hikers had been in awe of the opportunity to take a photo with such a great climber. But after that interaction, they were even more impressed with the famous man's grace and humility.

We may have reason to be proud of what the Lord has done through our lives, but we must be ever mindful of the source of our success. Without humility, the very confidence that carried us forward can become a catalyst for humiliation.

Be confident, be strong, but most of all, be humble.

> *"Two men went to the Temple to pray. One was a Pharisee, and the other was a despised tax collector. The Pharisee stood by himself and prayed this prayer: 'I thank you, God, that I am not like other people—cheaters, sinners, adulterers. I'm certainly not like that tax collector! I fast twice a week, and I give you a tenth of my income.'*
>
> *"But the tax collector stood at a distance and dared not even lift his eyes to heaven as he prayed. Instead, he beat his chest in sorrow, saying, 'O God, be merciful to me, for I am a sinner.' I tell you, this sinner, not the Pharisee, returned home justified before God. For those who exalt themselves will be humbled, and those who humble themselves will be exalted."*
>
> —Luke 18:10–14

PAUSE & PONDER:
RECORD YOUR REFLECTIONS AND PERSONAL INSIGHTS

When have you seen pride lead to a fall in your life or the life of someone you know? How can you continue to practice humility in your daily life?

Listen Up

"The crowd was listening."* This is how the Gospel of Luke describes a large crowd that had gathered to hear Jesus speak. Every preacher, teacher, lecturer, public speaker, and parent knows when the crowd is listening (and when they're not).

Hearing is not the same as *listening*. Hearing involves our ears, but listening engages our minds. For the person who hears, the speaker is background noise at best, while for the one who listens, the message resonates and reverberates throughout their being. When sounds become nouns, waveforms are transformed into meaning.

Jesus had the crowd's attention, and He used the opportunity to bring about clarity. Oftentimes, we don't need *more* information; we need *better* information. When information brings revelation, enlightenment is the outcome. It is only then that the crowd is truly "with" the speaker.

As He often did, Jesus used stories and illustrations to connect with His listeners. Stories and illustrations are masterful ways to bring concepts and ideas to life for those we hope to influence.

Jesus's story of the ten servants is a great example of the difference between hearing and listening. In the story, the servants all hear the same instructions; however, some of them are not listening. The nobleman instructs his servants to make an investment. He never encourages them to sit on what they have been given. Upon his return, most of the servants reply, "I invested." Pity the fool who sheepishly admits, "I hid."

If we shoot for nothing, we are certain to hit it. The Lord has given us many opportunities, abilities, gifts, and talents. Unfortunately, those blessings are all too often underutilized. We may have heard we have potential but somehow the message didn't resonate, and we squander the investment that was made in our lives. We fail to take it to heart. We fail to really listen.

The Lord is speaking. He is sharing insights and guidance in a variety of ways in order to show us how to maximize the investment He has made in our lives. Are we truly listening to the Lord? Are we investing what He's given us? If we are, we will reap the rewards.

While obedience in and of itself is always worth it, investing in the ways of the Lord also provides a high return on investment. God's ways don't disappoint. He has a reputation of exceeding expectations. Do you hear what I'm saying? Listen up!

The crowd was listening to everything Jesus said. And because he was nearing Jerusalem, he told them a story to correct the impression that the Kingdom of God would begin right away. He said, "A nobleman was called away to a distant empire to be crowned king and then return. Before he left, he called together ten of his servants and divided among them ten pounds of silver, saying, 'Invest this for me while I am gone.' But his people hated him and sent a delegation after him to say, 'We do not want him to be our king.'

"*After he was crowned king, he returned and called in the servants to whom he had given the money. He wanted to find out what their profits were. The first servant reported, 'Master, I invested your money and made ten times the original amount!'*

"*'Well done!' the king exclaimed. 'You are a good servant. You have been faithful with the little I entrusted to you, so you will be governor of ten cities as your reward.'*

"*The next servant reported, 'Master, I invested your money and made five times the original amount.'*

"*'Well done!' the king said. 'You will be governor over five cities.'*

"*But the third servant brought back only the original amount of money and said, 'Master, I hid your money and kept it safe. I was afraid because you are a hard man to deal with, taking what isn't yours and harvesting crops you didn't plant.'*

"'You wicked servant!' the king roared. 'Your own words condemn you. If you knew that I'm a hard man who takes what isn't mine and harvests crops I didn't plant, why didn't you deposit my money in the bank? At least I could have gotten some interest on it.'

"Then, turning to the others standing nearby, the king ordered, 'Take the money from this servant, and give it to the one who has ten pounds.'

"'But, master,' they said, 'he already has ten pounds!'

"'Yes,' the king replied, 'and to those who use well what they are given, even more will be given. But from those who do nothing, even what little they have will be taken away. And as for these enemies of mine who didn't want me to be their king— bring them in and execute them right here in front of me.'"

—Luke 19:11–27

PAUSE & PONDER:
RECORD YOUR REFLECTIONS AND PERSONAL INSIGHTS

What opportunities, abilities, gifts, and talents has God given you? How is He asking you to invest those?

DAY 35:

Walk the Talk

What is integrity? In its simplest form, integrity is doing what you say you will do. There's an old cowboy saying that goes like this: "Integrity is the distance between your mouth and your boots." Certainly, cowboys often met wranglers who could *talk the talk* but failed to *walk the talk*. They were "all hat and no cattle."

When I was a kid, my dad always had good intentions. One year, he promised to take my brother and me to Disneyland. I was so excited, and I looked forward to that trip for months. But despite all the talk, we never made it to Disney. Instead, Dad took us a few hours away to Six Flags in Arlington, Texas. We drove to and from the park in the same day, packing what should have been a kid's dream trip into one hot, rushed afternoon.

I can still see myself in our old blue Ford Galaxie 500 sedan as we drove down the highway with all the windows down, begging for cool air as we pressed on toward Six Flags. I can still feel that deep, gut-level disappointment. My dad had broken his word, yet again, and I was heartbroken.

My dad was a big talker, but his good intentions often fell short. He talked a good game, but he failed to walk the talk. That trip to Six Flags is just one example of the many times my dad didn't come through on a promise. His approach had a lasting impact on me as a young boy. It wounded our relationship and made me think I couldn't trust him.

I am certain my dad didn't want to hurt me. I loved my dad, but I determined at an early age not to follow his example. I would do my best to deliver on my good intentions. Those childhood experiences gave me a great appreciation for integrity—doing what you say you will do—and it's one of my top five values today. For me, good intentions are the enemy of integrity.

In today's world, there is no shortage of showmen—people who wave their hands and dazzle with words and charisma. They've got the *wow,* but they rarely show us *how.*

What about you? Do you do what you say you will do? Be a person of your word. Be on time. Keep your commitments. Do what you say you'll do, and look for ways to exceed expectations. That's what it looks like to walk the talk and live with integrity.

> *"But what do you think about this? A man with two sons told the older boy, 'Son, go out and work in the vineyard today.' The son answered, 'No, I won't go,' but later he changed his mind and went anyway. Then the father told the other son, 'You go,' and he said, 'Yes, sir, I will.' But he didn't go.*
>
> *"Which of the two obeyed his father?" They replied, "The first."*

Then Jesus explained his meaning: "I tell you the truth, corrupt tax collectors and prostitutes will get into the Kingdom of God before you do. For John the Baptist came and showed you the right way to live, but you didn't believe him, while tax collectors and prostitutes did. And even when you saw this happening, you refused to believe him and repent of your sins."

—Matthew 21:28–32

PAUSE & PONDER:
RECORD YOUR REFLECTIONS AND PERSONAL INSIGHTS

When was the last time you had good intentions but didn't follow through on what you said you would do? How can you live with more integrity in that area of your life?

Taking Advantage?

Some people make things happen while others simply watch and wait. Life is full of givers and takers, those who provide opportunity and those who are practicing opportunists.

Jesus tells a story about two types of farmers—a landowner and a group of tenant farmers. The landowner plants, builds, leases, and collects, while the other farmers grab, beat, kill, and stone. One provides an advantage, while the others take advantage.

In the story, the owner of the vineyard assumes that the tenant farmers will eventually do the right thing, despite their past violence. He says, *"Surely they will . . ."* Unfortunately, the owner is wrong, and the tenant farmers end up killing his son.

Change doesn't come easily. Especially if that change involves *us*. Unless the Lord does a work in our hearts, we will continue to do unjust things just as we always have.

However, God is sovereign, and He has a way of working things out according to His plan. In the end, God's standard of justice will prevail. The bar will not be lowered. Those who lack initiative and fail to take responsibility will not succeed. Those who take advantage of others will not be able to simply plow around the standard or ignore its presence. They will be measured against the perfect righteousness of Jesus, the cornerstone of our faith. They will feel the weight of God's demand for justice, and unless they embrace the cornerstone, they will be crushed by it.

Which type of person are you? Are you a giver or a taker? Are you looking out for others, or are you looking out for yourself? Are you providing opportunities, or are you working things to your advantage to get what you want? Do you stand in the gap, or do you stand by, complacent?

Pause and really think through your answers. Examine your motives, and ask God to show you if you're doing something to glorify Him or to glorify yourself. Ask yourself: "Why am I doing this? Whose interests am I representing?"

Beware of how you choose to answer those questions, or you might find yourself stumbling over the standard. Remember, the cornerstone will not be moved.

"Now listen to another story. A certain landowner planted a vineyard, built a wall around it, dug a pit for pressing out the grape juice, and built a lookout tower. Then he leased the vineyard to tenant farmers and moved to another country. At the time of the

grape harvest, he sent his servants to collect his share of the crop. But the farmers grabbed his servants, beat one, killed one, and stoned another. So the landowner sent a larger group of his servants to collect for him, but the results were the same.

"Finally, the owner sent his son, thinking, 'Surely they will respect my son.'

"But when the tenant farmers saw his son coming, they said to one another, 'Here comes the heir to this estate. Come on, let's kill him and get the estate for ourselves!' So they grabbed him, dragged him out of the vineyard, and murdered him.

"When the owner of the vineyard returns," Jesus asked, "what do you think he will do to those farmers?"

The religious leaders replied, "He will put the wicked men to a horrible death and lease the vineyard to others who will give him his share of the crop after each harvest."

Then Jesus asked them, "Didn't you ever read this in the Scriptures?

'The stone that the builders rejected
    has now become the cornerstone.
This is the Lord's doing,
    and it is wonderful to see.'

"I tell you, the Kingdom of God will be taken away from you and given to a nation that will produce the proper fruit. Anyone who stumbles over that stone will be broken to pieces, and it will crush anyone it falls on."

—Matthew 21:33–44

PAUSE & PONDER:
RECORD YOUR REFLECTIONS AND PERSONAL INSIGHTS

Are you manipulating people or situations to get what you want? Whose interests are you representing? How can you be a giver who stands in the gap for other people?

Hard-Hearted, Half-Hearted, or Wholehearted?

What gets your attention? What gains your interest beyond intrigue? What are the things that capture your dedication and devotion to the point that you will do whatever it takes not to miss out on an opportunity? What are you committed to?

Jesus tells a story about a generous king who throws a massive party. The king sends out many invitations, but much to his surprise, no one accepts. The invitations gain people's attention, but they will not commit.

Then the king broadens his invitation, and there is a considerable change in response. Many people come, but even then, some of the guests appear to be more intrigued than committed. They arrive fascinated but ill-prepared. The party guests fall into at least three categories: the hard-hearted, the half-hearted, and the wholehearted.

It is easier to ignore an invitation than to respond. It is easier to come at your convenience than to be counted upon. Commitment is a matter of the heart—it reveals what you value most. What garners your commitment gains your heart.

How do you decide what you will commit to? What relationships matter the most to you? In what areas of your life are you providing lip service rather than heartfelt loyalty? Are your commitments based on convenience and what you stand to get in return, or are they based on what you truly value?

Jesus invites us to the grand party He calls abundant life. He hopes we will respond to the external call with an internal commitment. He doesn't round us up and force us into confinement. Rather, He invites us to experience life with Him and to celebrate with a party at His place.

We have to decide, and we have to respond. The choice is ours. Where will we place our commitments? What friends, family members, and faith will gain our attention, garner our response, and receive our commitment?

> *"The Kingdom of Heaven can be illustrated by the story of a king who prepared a great wedding feast for his son. When the banquet was ready, he sent his servants to notify those who were invited. But they all refused to come!*
>
> *"So he sent other servants to tell them, 'The feast has been prepared. The bulls and fattened cattle have been killed, and everything is ready. Come to the banquet!' But the guests he had invited ignored them*

and went their own way, one to his farm, another to his business. Others seized his messengers and insulted them and killed them.

"The king was furious, and he sent out his army to destroy the murderers and burn their town. And he said to his servants, 'The wedding feast is ready, and the guests I invited aren't worthy of the honor. Now go out to the street corners and invite everyone you see.' So the servants brought in everyone they could find, good and bad alike, and the banquet hall was filled with guests.

"But when the king came in to meet the guests, he noticed a man who wasn't wearing the proper clothes for a wedding. 'Friend,' he asked, 'how is it that you are here without wedding clothes?' But the man had no reply. Then the king said to his aides, 'Bind his hands and feet and throw him into the outer darkness, where there will be weeping and gnashing of teeth.'

"For many are called, but few are chosen."
—Matthew 22:2–14

PAUSE & PONDER:
RECORD YOUR REFLECTIONS AND PERSONAL INSIGHTS

What's one area of your life where you're hard-hearted or half-hearted right now? What would it look like to move toward wholeheartedness?

Fig-ure It Out!

Take this one to the bank: There is a certain cause and effect at play in the world, and we would do well to watch, listen, and learn.

Jesus makes it clear that some things are as predictable as a fig tree's routine. There is a rhythm and order to the world that is far more complex than it might appear to be on the surface. For example, when a fig tree's buds become tender and its leaves begin to sprout, you can know that summer is on its way.

Jesus turns the corner on the fig tree metaphor and reminds His followers that there will come a day, preceded by obvious signs, when heaven and earth as we know it will simply disappear. What a sobering thought. Does nothing last forever?

There is one thing that endures the test of time: His Word. His Word lasts forever, and *He* is the Word. He was, is, and forever will be. The good news is that Jesus said He would go ahead of us and prepare a place so that we might be with Him forever. That's what I'm talking about. Count me in on that plan. So, how do we punch that ticket?

Jesus is the way to that forever-place. In Him and through Him, eternal life is found today. Not through the church, not through any efforts of our own, but through the One who made a way. Let's not miss the obvious. Watch, listen, and learn the way of the Lord, which is found only in relationship with Jesus. The answer is found in the words of Jesus in the Gospels—in the "red letters," if you will.

Jesus makes the cause and effect clear: Your choice—whether or not to follow him—impacts your life here and now as well as your life eternally. Recognize where your life is heading. Turn from your ways. Call on Jesus as Lord. Believe He is who He says He is, and accept Him as your Savior. Then you can rest assured, knowing your future is in His hands, today and forever. I pray you figure it out! All of heaven is praying that you will!

> *"Now learn a lesson from the fig tree. When its branches bud and its leaves begin to sprout, you know that summer is near. In the same way, when you see all these things, you can know his return is very near, right at the door. I tell you the truth, this generation will not pass from the scene until all these things take place. Heaven and earth will disappear, but my words will never disappear."*
>
> —Matthew 24:32–35

PAUSE & PONDER:
RECORD YOUR REFLECTIONS AND PERSONAL INSIGHTS

Do you tend to look to the church, your own efforts, or something other than Jesus to make you right with God? Ask Jesus to show you how He is the only way to a secure future with Him.

Aware and Prepared

Eligibility is no guarantee of acceptance. Being six foot four doesn't mean you'll automatically play center. Having an impressive résumé doesn't mean you'll get the job. Growing up in a Christian home doesn't equal being right with God.

With that reality in mind, it can sometimes seem like a waste of time to have your ducks in a row. What's the point when you can't control the outcome? However, since we don't always know when an opportunity will come knocking, it's important to be ready when the time comes.

In the parable of the ten bridesmaids, Jesus shows the importance of being aware and prepared. He does not tell us to worry. He does not say we should fret. But He does encourage us to be ready.

This parable reminds me of my father-in-law, Darrell. Darrell always encouraged his children to keep a one-hundred-dollar bill tucked away in their wallet and to never let the gas in their cars get below a quarter of a tank. More than once, I've reflected on his advice as I stood beside my vehicle with a red gasoline can in my hand, wishing I had listened. I've also had those same thoughts as I stood in a checkout lane only to discover I was short on cash. Those wise words lingered in my mind: "Be prepared." I wasn't!

We can count on God to do His part. The question is: Will we do ours? Are we ready for what might come our way today? Are we physically, mentally, emotionally, and spiritually fit to face the challenges life throws at us? If we are ready, we will be prepared to give our all when the time comes.

God is always present and working, and we can do all things through Christ who strengthens us. Not by our own might or power, but by the Spirit, says the Lord. Trust in Him. Lean not on your own understanding. Acknowledge Him, and He will direct you.

Are you ready? Be aware and prepared. Tuck away a bill, fill your tank, and be ready to take on the day. Let's do this!

"Then the Kingdom of Heaven will be like ten bridesmaids who took their lamps and went to meet the bridegroom. Five of them were foolish, and five were wise. The five who were foolish didn't take enough olive oil for their lamps, but the other five were wise enough to take along extra oil. When the bridegroom was delayed, they all became drowsy and fell asleep.

"At midnight they were roused by the shout, 'Look, the bridegroom is coming! Come out and meet him!'

"All the bridesmaids got up and prepared their lamps. Then the five foolish ones asked the others, 'Please give us some of your oil because our lamps are going out.'

"But the others replied, 'We don't have enough for all of us. Go to a shop and buy some for yourselves.'

"But while they were gone to buy oil, the bridegroom came. Then those who were ready went in with him to the marriage feast, and the door was locked. Later, when the other five bridesmaids returned, they stood outside, calling, 'Lord! Lord! Open the door for us!'

"But he called back, 'Believe me, I don't know you!'

"So you, too, must keep watch! For you do not know the day or hour of my return."

—Matthew 25:1–13

PAUSE & PONDER:
RECORD YOUR REFLECTIONS AND PERSONAL INSIGHTS

Are you aware of what God's doing in your life? How can you be more prepared physically, mentally, emotionally, and spiritually to face life's challenges?

DAY 40:

When Did We?

Everyone wants their life to matter. Everyone wants to know their life made a difference. But not everyone's life has impact. And more often it's not because they couldn't make an impact but because they chose not to.

A life that counts is lived by one who is on the lookout—watching and waiting for opportunities, large and small, to make a difference in the lives of people they encounter.

A life that fails to matter is lived by one who is always looking in, not out. Their focus is on the self. Personal wants and needs are all that matter, and others are left to fend for themselves. The impact of a self-centered life is no deeper than a dimple on a golf ball.

Jesus's teaching caused His followers to ask a list of *"When did we . . ."* questions. He told them that when they fed the hungry, helped the thirsty, housed the homeless, clothed the naked, cared for the sick, and visited the incarcerated, they also did those things for Him.

So, what about us? When did we? When it comes to opportunities to love other people, either we did, or we did not. Either way, it was a matter of the heart—our actions reflected the condition of our very soul.

What you do in life comes not just from who you are but also *whose* you are. Our actions are an outward expression of an inward condition. They are an indicator of a heart owned by another. A heart owned by Him. Knowing Jesus as Savior and letting Him lead your life impacts others as well as yourself, now and forever.

Are you His? Do you have your own list of *"When did we . . ."* questions? I hope so. If you are His, you will have a heart for Jesus that is seen through how you serve those who have the least to offer.

How sweet to someday hear Him say, *"When you did it to one of the least of these my brothers and sisters, you were doing it to me!"* Find one person you can serve today. When you do, rest assured you have in fact encountered the One. His name is Jesus.

> *"But when the Son of Man comes in his glory, and all the angels with him, then he will sit upon his glorious throne. All the nations will be gathered in his presence, and he will separate the people as a shepherd separates the sheep from the goats. He will place the sheep at his right hand and the goats at his left.*
>
> *"Then the King will say to those on his right, 'Come, you who are blessed by my Father, inherit the Kingdom prepared for you from the creation of the world. For*

I was hungry, and you fed me. I was thirsty, and you gave me a drink. I was a stranger, and you invited me into your home. I was naked, and you gave me clothing. I was sick, and you cared for me. I was in prison, and you visited me.'

"Then these righteous ones will reply, 'Lord, when did we ever see you hungry and feed you? Or thirsty and give you something to drink? Or a stranger and show you hospitality? Or naked and give you clothing? When did we ever see you sick or in prison and visit you?'*

"And the King will say, 'I tell you the truth, when you did it to one of the least of these my brothers and sisters, you were doing it to me!'*

"Then the King will turn to those on the left and say, 'Away with you, you cursed ones, into the eternal fire prepared for the devil and his demons. For I was hungry, and you didn't feed me. I was thirsty, and you didn't give me a drink. I was a stranger, and you didn't invite me into your home. I was naked, and you didn't give me clothing. I was sick and in prison, and you didn't visit me.'*

"Then they will reply, 'Lord, when did we ever see you hungry or thirsty or a stranger or naked or sick or in prison, and not help you?'*

"And he will answer, 'I tell you the truth, when you refused to help the least of these my brothers and sisters, you were refusing to help me.'

"And they will go away into eternal punishment, but the righteous will go into eternal life."
—Matthew 25:31–46

PAUSE & PONDER:
RECORD YOUR REFLECTIONS AND PERSONAL INSIGHTS

Write down three ways you can serve other people this week. Try to think of people who can't pay you back.

Acknowledgments

Thanks be to the greatest storyteller who ever lived, sweet Jesus, my Lord and Savior and the One who has forever changed my life.

This little book would have never come to life without the unwavering encouragement of my dear family and friends. Jesus has been so good to us. He has made us who we are and who we hope to be. I hope I have made you proud. To God be the glory! I love you all!

To the love of my life, Stephanie. You have always believed in me, encouraged me, and loved me unconditionally. Thanks for letting Jesus use you in my life.

To my wonderful children, Lauren-Elaine, Olivia-Christine, Joshua, Isaac, Emily-Rose, and Sophia-Rae, you have taught me more about life than you will ever know. Special thanks to my daughter-in-law Makenzy for being a second set of eyes! And to the grandbabies, you bring Papa Bear so much joy! I pray you will learn great life lessons as you turn the pages of this book.

To my mother, Patsy Ann. You have been the anchor through many storms. Your love never fails. I am forever grateful you chose life!

To my friends, Randy Davis, Brian Banks, Michael Catt, Dr. Anthony Jordan, Dr. Robert Haskins, Doug Coe, Tim Coe, David Coe, Marty Sherman, Jim Hiskey, Tim Burchfield,

Dave Gillogly, Oliver and Anita Powers, I am who I am because each of you has invested your life in me. Thanks for your encouragement.

For all of you who have uttered these words: "You need to share your thoughts about the parables in a book." What in the world was I thinking? Now you know! And maybe we have learned more about what Jesus was thinking too! Thank you for helping make the dream come true.

About the Author

Ray Sanders is the founder and CEO of Coaching Leaders, an executive coaching and revenue-generating business consulting firm that partners with Fortune 500 executives, CEOs, entrepreneurs, and business owners to help them navigate the challenges and opportunities that come with growing their companies and strengthening their leadership teams (raysanders.com).

As a CEO, Ray has grown multimillion-dollar organizations, advanced national and international brands, led a financial institution, served in a nonpartisan role with the United States Senate, led print and broadcast organizations, and pioneered initiatives to bring clean water to remote regions of the world. His leadership experience spans more than forty years.

Ray is recognized by his peers as a leader of leaders, a whiteboard aficionado, and an innovative growth strategist with a passion for purpose-driven cultures and values-based leadership development. His business coaching, mentoring, and personal ministry have given him a unique perspective on the wide range of struggles leaders face in all walks of life.

A skilled communicator, Ray has served as editor in chief for Oklahoma's largest weekly news journal, hosted an award-winning radio program, and been a keynote speaker for conventions, conferences, and campuses. He has published more than 150 articles and feature stories in print and online publications, including The Baptist Messenger, The Oklahoman, the Oklahoma Press Association, and others. Ray holds a BA degree from the University of Oklahoma.

Ray and his wife, Stephanie, are the founders of Edify Leaders, a nonprofit organization that inspires and mobilizes leaders to use their influence to impact the world for good (edifyleaders.org). While Ray continues to lead a thriving business in the marketplace, he also dedicates much of his time to speaking and leading ministry coaches who encourage hundreds of ministry leaders as they navigate the challenges of life and ministry.

A world traveler, Ray enjoys exploring new places with the love of his life, Stephanie. Together, they have six grown children and ten grandchildren.

www.ingramcontent.com/pod-product-compliance
Lightning Source LLC
Chambersburg PA
CBHW051426090426
42737CB00014B/2844